THIEVES
ON
WALL
STREET

By

Gunther Karger

Discovery Group Inc.
Reno, Nevada

Printed in the United States of America

Book Design by Gunther Karger
Illustration by Eduardo Ramirez
Cover by Humberto Santano

Published by Discovery Group Incorporated
1280 Terminal Way, Suite 3
Reno, Nevada 89502

ISBN: 0-9645979-1-8
Library of Congress

DISCLAIMER

This book is sold with the express understanding that the publisher is not engaged in rendering legal advise nor recommending the purchase or sale of securities. The information herein is believed to be reliable at the time it was written, but it cannot be guaranteed insofar as it applies to any particular situation or individual. The intent of this book is to present processes and practices in place within the securities industry at the time this is written and it should be recognized that these are subject to change over time.

Any close similarity between examples given and actual cases is purely coincidental and the Publisher and Author clearly disclaim any responsibility arising from such potential coincidental similarities. The publisher specifically disclaims any liability, loss or risk incurred directly or indirectly as a consequence of using the information contained herein.

The publisher, author or distributors of this book will not under any circumstances be liable to the purchaser for any amount greater than the purchase price of this book.

ALSO BY GUNTHER KARGER

Your Plan To Success
Communications in the Year 2000
International Spacelog
The Discovery Letter

"Opportunity makes the thief"
English Proverb

"An eggthief becomes a camelthief"
Persian Proverb

"When money speaks, truth keeps silent"
Russian Proverb

*"My son, let them not depart from your eyes.
Keep sound wisdom and discretion. Then, you will walk
safely in your way and your foot will not stumble."*

The Holy Bible, Book of Proverbs

i

DEDICATION

I dedicate this book to Shirley, my wife of 40 years who stood by and watched the *Thieves* while I applied logic to how the system should work but didn't. Her constant encouragement led me to write this book in the hope that some good can come of it. Thanks to her unrelenting encouragement and substantial help along the way, here come the *Thieves On Wall Street*.

I also dedicate this book to all the investors who have trusted a system which has not dealt fairly with them. It is incredulous how, in this modern age, it has been possible for so many street professionals and their firms to have been allowed to get away with all that has been seen for so long. It is my hope, through this book, that the individual investor will better understand how the securities industry **really** works and how their odds can be improved.

I also dedicate this book to my parents, Herbert and Ida Karger, who selflessly sacrificed their lives by smuggling me out of Germany in late 1939 so that I could live to accomplish this humble task.

I pray, in their memory, that if this book helps just one investor even in a small way, my presence in this World, thanks to their sacrifice, has done some good.

Gunther Karger
May, 1995

ACKNOWLEDGEMENTS

I thank my publisher, Discovery Group Inc. for making it possible to complete this project from start to first printing in seven months.

I thank Shirley, my wife, for working with me closely, reading and re-reading and making valuable suggestions. She was especially helpful as we have worked side by side for so many years and also met many of the *Thieves* along the way.

Carol Accornero as the principal lay reader brought forward valuable suggestions and I am deeply grateful for her help.

Eduardo Ramirez and Humberto Santano contributed to the illustration and cover design which appropriately set the tone for this book.

I must especially recognize Shoshana Kurzweil whose music based on the Scriptures stimulated my motivation to complete this project.

Lastly, I thank my parents, in memoriam, for my opportunity to live so that I could complete this work. Not having seen them since I was six, I look forward to the day when I can personally deliver this book to them in a higher world free of *Thieves*.

Gunther Karger
May, 1995

INTRODUCTION

This book is about **Wall Street**. Where it is. How it works. The brokerage industry. *Thieves on Wall Street* reaches into the inner sanctum of the *stock market* and tells you how it **really** works. This entire book is about how all this affects **you**, the individual investor and what you can do about it to still make money.

This book is organized to achieve **six goals**:

1. **Defines** what the market is and where it is.
2. **Tells** you all about the securities industry, how it operates and presents this in a way that you can understand.
3. **Tells** you how markets and stocks are manipulated for the benefit of a few and who they are.
4. **Tells** you about market makers, traders, bear raids, penny stocks, boiler rooms and much more.
5. **Gives** you **The Investor's Survival Guide** which tells you how to protect your money from commission hungry brokers and shows you specific actions you **can** take to **still make money**.
6. **Presents** a prescription to change the system for the better.

This book is written for you, the **individual** investor. To give you a better chance of making money despite all that goes on in the stock market.

Thieves on Wall Street

TABLE OF CONTENTS

PREFACE

This book is about the world of investments. The real world of the securities industry. It takes you **inside** to corners rarely, if ever visited. This world is made up of people. Human beings like you and me. People who breathe, eat, sleep, have joys and sorrows.

Most of us are honest and wouldn't dream of stealing anything from anyone. We usually work in industries and situations that make it very difficult for us to even try.

But there are industries that operate in a way making it difficult for individuals to be totally honest.

Take a car salesman for instance. Typically, the car dealer has hired an army of sales people working seven days each week from morning to night including holidays. This person gets paid only if there is a sale and usually only when the sale is made at a price giving the dealer a profit. When a customer walks through the door, there is a rush by at least a dozen salespeople to greet this customer. If the salesperson is lucky, the customer buys the car, after lots of haggling about price and conferences with the sales manager. The salesperson may get anywhere from $25 to $500 commission depending on how much haggling is done and how low a price the manager is willing to take just to get the sale. It probably will be the only sale that day for that salesperson. It may be the only sale that week. How honest would you say this salesperson is? Would he tell you **anything** he needed to say to make you buy that car? Especially a used car? Even if it stretched his most creative imagination?

After you bought the used car from that salesperson and you found it misrepresented, would you call him a **thief** and **conman**? Alternatively, would you call the **system** he worked in faulty?

This is the world of **commissioned sales.** You eat if you sell and starve and get fired if you don't. Sometimes, the company offers some training. Often, it doesn't. The company sets **your** sales goals. You either make your goal or get fired! You also get a bonus if you exceed your sales goal. It's up to you to make it in any way you can. How is that for temptation and motivation?

The company has rules you are asked to follow. The most important rule is to meet your sales goals and do whatever it takes to achieve this goal. That's how you make money and the company prospers. That's how you keep your job, if you work in the brokerage industry.

Sometimes, there are laws regulating how you sell and how your company conducts its business. The most important law of all is to achieve your goals, within the law and company rules, if **possible.** You are encouraged to reach into your brain for the creativity you need to guide you into the deep reaches of your customers pockets. The one rule you know is:

The bigger the sale, the bigger is your pay

Now, let's get back to the world of investments. Brokers, brokerage firms, mutual funds, limited partnerships, derivatives and investment banks. That's what this book is about. How the people and companies in this industry operate. How they make their money. Some of them make fortunes. Billions of Dollars.

There was a most respected titan of Wall Street known as **king of the bond world** who made a billion Dollars in just one year. When he entered a room, people stood in awe and bowed. He was great. He was King. Then, it was realized that the billion he made came from people like you and me. A Court even ruled him to be a **thief** and he went to jail.

Yes, he was very creative and lived by the rules of his company and industry. He just was one of the very few who got caught. Now, even after having lived in executive prison and paid more than $500 million in fines, he still has a fortune worth hundreds of millions and lives a life of splendor.

That's how the system works. The more creative you are, the more you make and the better chance you have not only to make a reasonable living, but a chance to get **rich**. If you want to work in this business you have to live within the **system**. You also have to live with yourself knowing what you must do to survive and make a decent living.

Is there any protection against potential abuse in the investment and securities world?

There is the National Association of Securities Dealers (NASD) that is established as the **self regulating** arm of this industry. Its members are the brokerage firms that pay for the expenses to operate the NASD.

Each person desiring to become a broker must take a test administered by the NASD and adhere to its rules.

We have the Securities and Exchange Commission (SEC), a government agency whose chairman reports to the President. This agency typically is staffed by senior executives from the securities industry who return to that industry in a more senior position than he had with the government.

Yes, there is some supervision. But with nearly one half million registered brokers and countless others who somehow operate as brokers, there is ample opportunity for extraordinary creativity. Creativity in developing new products, sales techniques and schemes that surface over time. How much good can the SEC really do with an enforcement budget of less than $50 million annually?

One year, we identify the **penny stock brokers** as the scam artists and go after them. The next year, we find the **junk bond creators** who destroy fine companies and put millions of workers out of work.

Then, we focus on the **insider traders** who take undue advantage of early information **before** we, the ordinary folk have the slightest chance. Next we blame the **limited partnerships** that fleeced billions from the public.

Recently, we learned about the **derivatives** that reduced corporate earnings thus hitting the wallets of investors through lower stock prices. We have computerized stock trading systems that move the stock market up and down like a roller coaster for reasons having little or nothing to do with investment fundamentals. We have boiler rooms full of telemarketing personnel selling partnerships in non-existing wireless cable TV systems.

All of these products, techniques and systems were developed, approved and offered by **Wall Street**. This includes Wall Street's companies, their big bosses and heads of their compliance and due diligence departments. I mention the **Compliance** and **Due Diligence** departments because each brokerage firm is required to have these departments to ensure that each firm and all brokers within the company comply with the regulations. These regulations are in place to protect **your** interest. You saw them advertised in the most respected financial publications. The companies creating and sponsoring them were and still are the most respected firms on Wall Street.

How do these companies and people make their money? By selling to you, the individual investor. The bigger the sale and the more they sell, the more money they make. The more imaginative and creative they get, the more they make. The bigger the investment is, the bigger is **your risk.**

Lets look at three mega-examples of what can happen when Wall Street lets loose the most creative of the **Street Folk**.

KIDDER PEABODY was one of the biggest Wall Street Firms owned by corporate giant General Electric. An obscure trader amassed $9 million in commissions by trading more than one **trillion Dollars** of Government Bonds before someone woke up and realized it wasn't for real. This lead to the end of that firm when General Electric sold it to another Wall Street Giant, Paine Webber.

Late February 1995, **Barings Bank** failed after 250 years, having financed the Louisiana Purchase by The Unites States and serving the British Royal family's banking needs for centuries. What happened? A 28 year old rogue trader bought derivatives betting that the stocks on the Tokyo Exchange**(Nikkei)** would rise. He placed his bet on the **wrong** side of that market. The **Nikkei** fell instead and **Barings Bank** lost a cool $900 million Dollars overnight. This was more capital than the bank had and the British banking officials took over BARINGS which ceased to exist instantly.

Whose money did these people play with and lose? Why **yours**, of course. The investors who owned the bank and those who invested in the bank's financial products. Making it worse still, the day after BARING'S collapse, the MEXICAN BOLSA exchange dropped another 100 points and the Tokyo **Nikkei** fell several hundred points. Who owns shares trading on these and other exchanges? You do. Because many of you owned shares of international mutual funds that dropped significantly on this event.

All because of a 28 year old kid who was creative, very greedy and yes, **very unsupervised**. By the way, he vanished from the face of the Earth within a day of this international banking disaster.

A major mutual fund disclosed, early in 1995, a huge **$2 Billion mistake** blamed on a computer entry error by a bookkeeper. This dramatically reduced the dividend paid to the investors. That's you!

Solomon, one of Wall Street's most respected brokerage and investment banking firms, disclosed in February 1995 that it was incurring charges of $175 million resulting from "**botched up bookkeeping** on its trading desk," as reported by the Wall Street Journal on February 28, 1995. Just the previous day, it was reported that this very same firm announced the reclassification of $510 million in revenues.

Who lost in this? If you held shares in Solomon, you lost 2.4% in just one day, the very day when the DOW rose past the historic 4000 mark. Where was the supervision? What were the Vice Presidents making $100,000 plus bonuses yearly doing? How could this happen with the advanced computers supporting every function of business in the 90's?

Now, lets get back to the brokers, their products and you, the investor and their client.

Do they want to make you money as well? Of course! Some of us have made money. But, whether we win or lose, the companies and people of the securities industry make money because the system is transaction based. Whatever we buy, we must sell. And, whether we buy or sell, there is a transaction commission. This gives the securities industry a tremendous incentive for stimulating activity.

The purpose of this book is not to suggest that everyone working in the investment business is a sleazy thief. Very much to the contrary, most of the people are hard working and just want to make a reasonable living at what they do.

But a living they must make and there is ample opportunity for **imagination and greed** within the system they work. The opportunity for great gain exists on both sides. On the side of the investor as well as the investment professional and his company. However, the cards are grossly stacked against the individual investor.

The purpose of this book is to present how the system **really** works. It is the author's belief that this understanding can give the individual investor a much better chance of also making money. Importantly, this understanding can help the investor to avoid potential situations which are likely to result in losses up to and including life savings. Failure to adequately understand how Wall Street works can lead to serious illness and occasionally even death.

Is this book only about brokers and the securities industry? **Definitely not!** As you travel through the chapters, you will meet bankers, financial planners, magazine and newspaper editors, financial commentators on radio and TV, high level government agencies and its administrators. You will even meet company presidents and in one instance, the President of the United States. These are the people in the industry we call **Investments** and **Securities**.

This book is about a **system** that's structured to work with **your** money and is principally transaction oriented. This book tells you what you **can do** in your defense and even make money in spite of all the hands reaching out to your pocket.

       INVESTMENT: An outlay of money for gain and profit
       SECURITY: An obligation to protect, assure, pledge and commit

WHERE IS
WALL STREET?

Wall Street is a street in New York's financial district, the home of the New York Stock Exchange, the American Stock Exchange and other financial institutions.

Wall Street is where brokerage houses are headquartered whether it be the large Merrill Lynch tower in New York or a broker dealer operating out of a one room loft in a small southern town.

Wall Street is in Chicago, the home of the futures exchanges and the center of world commodity trading. Chicago has been made famous(other than the Great Chicago Fire and the Chicago Bears) as the World Hq. for the commodity pits. This is where a bunch of people mill around large rooms and yell at each other all day. The waving of their hands and their shouts could spell fortune or disaster for humble people like ourselves. This is where Hillary Rodham Clinton made her first fortune kissing the tail of cattle futures traders whose yells put $100,000 in Hillary's pocket.

Wall Street is in Los Angeles, the home of the Pacific Stock Exchange and Denver which was the original home of the *Penny Stock Brokers.* You can find **Wall Street** in Singapore, London, Frankfurt, Moscow and yes, even in Bejing. Before we forget, I must mention Vancouver, the home of the seething Canadian mining stock exchange.

"Wall Street" is even closer than your broker's office, even if his office is just down the street. **Wall Street** is your newspaper, TV, computer and yes, your telephone.

Wall Street comes to you in the airplane, on your boat and in your car. Wherever there is a phone or radio receiver.

Oops, I almost forgot! Your bank. And that's important. The most important place of all. That's where your money is. Haven't you noticed? The bank lobby now has a desk right by he door. A desk called **investments.** Your friendly bank has made it easy to get and keep your money. It wants to get a piece of the action.

Have I missed any place **Wall Street** has invaded? You bet! The flea market. Where you go to sell your rags and used stuff. You probably will find a stand ready to accept the proceeds from your sale to invest in mutual funds, limited partnerships, insurance and **deals** you might only find at flea markets.

Yes, **Wall Street** is everywhere and it reaches out for your wallet and savings. Be sure you know this street's map before you wander into it and get lost.

Wall Street is everywhere.

WHAT IS
THE MARKET?

What is the **market**? What is its purpose? How does it function? Where is it? Who runs it? How do you, the investor, fit into it? How can the **market** possibly drain your wallet? How can you still use the **market** to your advantage?

Read on! You are about to learn things you never imagined.

Think about your favorite flea market. A place to buy and sell almost everything. What's the most important thing about the flea market? Pricing! Pricing is extremely flexible.

If you are a **seller**, you can charge whatever the market is willing to pay. And that depends mainly on the size of your mouth, your brain's ingenuity and your ability to size up your customer. If you are a buyer, you can and should offer less than you are willing to pay. The price you offer can be vastly different from the price asked by the seller. Never prejudge the final price at a flea market.

Your offer is limited only by your boldness or shyness, depending on what type of person you are. This has to do with your patience level, your urgency to buy or sell and the weather. Your success at the flea market also depends on your understanding of what your **eyes see, what your ears hear and what your brain understands.**

Your options are very simple. If you buy it, you got what you saw at the price negotiated and agreed to between **buyer** and **seller**. Once you bought or sold it, you either have it or you got rid of it. If later you believe that you made a mistake and needed the thing you sold after all, you either go back to the flea market or to the store to buy another.

You probably will pay more for it than what you sold it for because your need is greater and the urgency level is increased.

On the other hand, if you bought it and decided you didn't want it or it wasn't quite what you wanted, you could go back to the flea market to sell it for whatever you can get. You probably will get less for it than the price you paid.

Well, the **stock market** is like the flea market. Things are bought and sold for the prices buyers and sellers are willing to buy and sell. Whatever the laws of **flea market** allow, you can bet your money that these also apply to the **stock market**. I am very sure that the few laws that do exist are frequently stretched, just as they are at the flea market.

Think of the **stock market** in terms of a flea market. If you are a buyer, assume that you are about to be taken, unless you have good knowledge about what you are buying, its quality, price and safety. If you are a **dealer**, you size up the **mark** and give him the highest possible price you think you can get away with, using all the tricks of the trade. Just as there are many good opportunities at the flea market, there are opportunities also in the stock market. If you trusted your broker and financial institution equally to your trust in a flea market dealer, you probably would make good money in the stock market.

The financial world has several kinds of **markets**. I will describe the major markets so that you will understand them better. While reading about these markets, you should constantly keep in mind that these are systems and organizations structured to serve the securities industry. What is the one thing the entire securities industry depends upon? Transactions, commissions and fees to the companies for issuing stock. The industry will do almost anything possible and imaginable to increase its income from these services.

Since the whole system is designed and operated by the securities industry and policed by the National Association Securities Dealers, the NASD, the cards are heavily **stacked against the individual.**

If you are not very careful, this industry will reach out and touch you right in your pocket. Unfortunately, this hand will not necessarily enrich you. To the contrary, this hand could put you in the poor house very fast.

Elsewhere in this book, I will cover specific ways the brokerage industry **reaches into your pockets,** how the system works and how you can defend your wallet and protect your own profits.

Now, let's move to the exchanges. The market place of our financial world.

STOCK EXCHANGES

The **stock market** consists of Exchanges and broker dealers linked together in a giant computer network spanning the United States. Stock Exchanges like the New York Stock Exchange on Wall Street, The American Stock Exchange, Pacific Stock Exchange and others in the Unites States and in most financial centers around the world. These are highly computerized operations linking brokers together for a very efficient system. You can buy or sell a stock or bond in seconds.

The New York Stock Exchange alone handles 250 million transactions on an average day. Think about going to an auction but it is a thousand miles away in New York. You have a stock you want to sell and you know that the New York auction will find a buyer who is willing to pay a price. But wait! You don't have to go to New York after all. Just call your stock broker and tell him to give it to the New York auctioneer, since his office is connected to the main auction floor in New York. He is glad to get it sold for you if you pay his commission.

Think about stock exchanges as a **giant electronic auction** with specialists assigned to stocks and bidding between themselves. Just remember that the commission you pay him covers his pay, the expense for his office and the 10,000 people working in the main New York office taking up a whole skyscraper in the heart of the financial district otherwise known as Wall Street.

NASDAQ

Now, we come to the vast NASDAQ. The electronic stock quotation system operated by the National Association of Securities Dealers (NASD). Before computers came to our desks, this was called **Over the Counter** or the **Unlisted** market.

The NASDAQ is a giant **marketplace** where everything is **negotiated** between dealers unlike the Exchanges where everything is **auctioned**.

This is a vast network of communications linking all the dealers together via huge computers. When you visit your broker's office, you see a computer screen with lots of flashing numbers. This is usually the QUOTRON or some version doing the same thing. Stock prices are continually updated, upwards of 50,000 stocks plus futures, options, bonds derivatives, indexes and things that could boggle your mind.

Some NASDAQ brokers just use this system to get prices and call in their orders. Some brokers are also **dealers** sometimes known as **market makers** or **traders**. These people place **bids** indicating what price they are willing to pay for a given number of shares of a specific stock, bond or other type of security.

Conversely, they also place on this system their **offer** to buy or sell securities at a given price and the number of shares at that price.

All members of the NASDAQ system can see this information and thus get a good picture of the market for any given security at a given time. Just like a flea market, except this is the stock market and it's done on computers, worldwide and in every city and most villages in the USA.

Just like at the flea market, the investor using this system, through his broker, is at the mercy of the system including all the hungry dealers, brokers, market makers, traders, institutions. Everything goes, within the limits of the securities laws and the regulations of the NASD.

This is a **marketplace** where stocks and other financial instruments are bought and sold on a **negotiated** basis. This is unlike the exchanges which operate on the **auction** principle. The buying and selling of stocks is subject to rules set by the SEC and the NASD. These laws and rules often are stretched to the benefit of the securities professionals and their firms. Rarely to the benefit of you, the investor.

Before leaving the subject of the NASD, we should know that this organization, located in Maryland requires all brokerage firms to be a member, all brokers to be registered and licensed by the NASD.

Moreover, all brokers must work for a NASD approved member firm. The NASD is designated to be the **self regulating** body of the industry. It's job is to monitor the activities of all member firms(brokerage companies) and its brokers to make sure that the public is protected. Guess what? Who pays for this watchdog agency?

The brokers and their firms, of course. The same is for the futures industry that is served by the National Futures Association, based in Chicago. To whom do you think these self regulating agencies are most loyal?

I wouldn't be surprised if they favor those who pay a significant portion of NASD'S expenses and salaries for the use of the electronic system and supporting services. I don't imply herein that this is intentionally done to put the investor at an unfair disadvantage. This happens naturally because of the way the financial services industry is structured.

PINK SHEETS

The **Pink Sheets** represent a market that facilitates the buying and selling of stocks **not qualifying** for **NASDAQ** listing. The "pink sheets" is nothing more than a list of publicly traded **non Nasdaq qualified** stocks with prices they could have sold for during the prior month. These prices are not necessarily the real prices representing actual execution. The dealers simply provide their prices to the publisher of the listing and can give nearly any price they want. This is called **Pink Sheets** because the color of the paper is pink. Consider this market to be the **lowest** level of securities trading. In flea market terms, it's the area of the flea market where the ground is unpaved, the stands have no tops and the products are most questionable.

FUTURES EXCHANGES

We have the **futures** exchanges which in the United States are centered in Chicago. These often are called the **pits** where floor traders stand around a floor yelling like crazy, throwing up hands and pointing fingers.

This is the marketplace for hogs, grains, gasoline, heating oil, currencies, rice and things you would never imagine. Here, traders buy and sell contracts for future deliveries based on what the **Market** is willing to pay **Today** for the commodities. They even trade exotic things like **Bets** on where the stocks in New York and Japan are headed. These **bets** sometimes are called derivatives.

When you think about the futures markets, think about **derivatives** and how an aggressive county treasurer with the help of the biggest brokerage firm bankrupted one of the richest and largest counties in the U.S., Orange County, California early in 1995.

PRIVATE MARKETS

The previous markets above are the primary securities markets in the U.S. Other markets such as the INSTA-NET allows institutions to trade among themselves, often at much more favorable terms than is available to the individual investor. There is the private market where individuals and corporations make deals between themselves and nearly totally circumvent the brokerage industry. If you can tap into this one, you are lucky because this is where you can get the fairest deal. But don't count on this one as too many road blocks are placed in your way and very few securities are traded in this manner.

WHO ARE THE THIEVES ON WALL STREET?

This book is about **Thieves**. A special kind of thief. You could encounter this thief anytime and anywhere. This thief could be a man or woman you meet in person. Someone on the phone calling you. This is the most dangerous thief of all because you won't recognize him(or her) as a thief. The person calling could be a total stranger or someone you know very well.

In modern technocratic language, this thief has a high degree of **Stealth**. The U.S. Air Force has aircraft called stealth Fighters and bombers. These have **stealth** characteristics because they are invisible to the enemy radars. This aircraft can make a bombing run and the first the enemy knows about it is when the bomb explodes. The kind of thief we discuss in this book has similar characteristics. You won't recognize him until he has already come onto you, stolen from you and fled to legal sanctuary.

Where are you likely to encounter this thief? In your bank, the stock brokerage office, the other person when your phone rings and yes, even when you turn on your computer.

Wait! I forgot the TV and your favorite newspaper and magazine. Thieves advertise. They even send you letters.

THIEF: A person who steals, robs, defrauds, swindles, rips off, takes

Is there any **sanctuary from these thieves?** Not really. You might even meet them in your place of worship in the guise of a fellow worshipper or the representative of a higher being preaching to his flock wisdom and goodness.

Here is the bad news. These thieves steal from lots of people and rarely go to jail. They very rarely go to trial and hardly ever see the inside of a police station. Yet, they keep on stealing from you.

It gets worse. Most of the time you don't even know you have been the victim. You feel more empty. Your life has worsened economically because you have less money. But you don't look at it as having been victimized by a thief. In fact, you often blame yourself for having made poor decisions.

Sadly, these thieves could cause serious personal tragedies such as loss of home, divorce, deteriorating health and yes, even suicide. Visits by these thieves could even lead a person to a life of crime and eventually to jail.

Who are these thieves? How can you spot them so you have a chance to run the other way? Why aren't these people in jail? How can they get away with this?

These thieves have several things in common. First, they are **after your money.** Money you earn at work. Money you have saved and money you have won big at the lottery. When a company lays off people, like so often is happening these days of re-structuring, re-engineering and efficiency building, these thieves will especially look up the people just having received the **pink slip.**

A favorite place these thieves scour for victims is the obituary column. Because insurance and inheritance money is about to flow to the bereaved family members and it's money they are after.

How can you spot them? Here are a few hints. They usually are well dressed. Men in suits and ties. Women in smart business attire. They sit behind computers with flashing numbers moving rapidly and constantly across the screens.

When they call on the phone, they have smooth voices with a very convincing proposition. When you see them advertise, **them** can be in the guise of a major corporation well known to you. Yes, names that are household common.

When you see their ads and when you hear their voices, there is a common message. This message is the same whether a very professional person talks with you in person, you see someone on TV or when the phone rings.

They all want to make you money. Some are more conservative than others by offering you millionaire status by the time you retire. Others are more aggressive and offer you riches in a short time. Some even tell you that they can help you increase your wealth by 1000 percent in a few months.

Why are these people so eager to make you money? How can they be called thieves when all they want to do is to make you rich? What they do is legal and even supervised by the federal and state governments.

Very simple! They get paid commissions every time they get you to **invest** with them. Invest in **their** favorite things. Mutual funds, stocks, limited partnerships, bonds, derivatives, financial hedges and commodities. Commodities can offer the greatest rewards of all, according to these people. Even our First Lady made $100,000 in trading cattle futures. A former Speaker of the House made good side change by getting great advice on **new issues** otherwise known as Initial Public Offerings(IPO'S).

The more you invest with them, the more **they** make. Importantly, the more **times** you do business with these people, the more they make. It has to do with number and size of transactions. They have a strong incentive to get you to invest with them.

If they don't get enough of **your** money and the money of lots of people like yourself, their bosses will warn them to do **better** or face being **fired** for low production.

Who are these people? Some are called Stock Brokers. Others are known as Account Executives. Then there are Financial Planners and Financial Consultants. When they do well at getting your money, they move up the ladder and are called Vice President - Investments. If you are a corporation or bank trust officer, they become **Senior Vice President-Investments.**

These are the people of Wall Street. They are everywhere. In fancy offices. In bare offices partitioned off with small cubicles and sit by a telephone with a headset making 100 cold calls per day (sometimes known as boiler rooms). They work out of their homes. They sit at investment desks in bank lobbies.

Are all these people bad and just out for your money? Not at all. Most of them are very dedicated, highly trained and really do want you to make money with the investment they sell. But they only **sell**. That's their job.

The products they sell are devised by someone else. It could be a stock of a very good company or a company about to go bankrupt. They could suggest a bond paying a guaranteed dividend every month but not knowing that interest rates could rise steadily for the next 3 years and the bond you just bought could lose 50% of its value. It could be a mutual fund that the broker's company manages and is pushing by giving the broker a higher commission.

The broker could strongly be suggesting a stock just recommended by his research department in a fancy research report. What he may not know is that his company, through its investment banking department just received 100,000 shares of XYZ corporation as part of fees received for a service rendered. Now, the brokerage firm needs to move this stock out of its inventory and convert it to cash.

All the broker knows is that the company is sound, as stated in the research report and that he needs to sell lots of shares to meet his monthly quota for his bonus. He might have to push this stock on his clients just to keep his job. The pressure is intense for a broker to produce.

What about you? You are the investor who put up your money. What happens to you when you bought the wrong investment? **You could lose your money.** Money you worked hard for. Money you needed for your retirement.

The broker, his office manager and his company made money whether you did so or not because they received commission on each transaction. This commission comes from the transaction whether you buy or sell and whether you make or lose money.

Did the broker and Wall Street want you to make money? Of Course! The more you make, the more Wall Street makes. But who takes the risk? You take the whole risk. If you make a mistake, you pay. If you complain about not being told all the facts, you are told that it is **your responsibility** to fully investigate each investment. This is a truthful stark reality.

But you **trusted** the person in a fine suit, sitting in a fancy office and backed by a billion Dollar corporation in the heart of Wall Street. Still you paid.

Can you make money? Of course you can. You have to work hard and diligently in sorting out the myriad of investment products and understanding the behavior of the markets. This is difficult, complex and time consuming.

Often, the markets and prices of individual stocks are manipulated by a few very innovative brokers and investment professionals, for their excessive profits and at **your** expense. The individual investor stands little chance when exposed to this.

What about the Regulators and the Government's roles in protecting the investor? Yes, there is the NASD that supervises and licenses most sales persons in the investment industry. But who pays the salary and expenses of the NASD? The Brokerage industry! It self regulates itself.

What about the Government? The Federal Government has the Securities and Exchange Commission and each state has its Banking and Securities Secretariats.

Yes, when you invest and lose, you really have lost that money. You invested $100 and received $75 two years later when you sold it, for a $25 loss. Who made a profit from this transaction? The great people of the securities industry. They received commission when you bought and also, when you sold. Are they thieves? No! Not by the standard definition of what a thief is.

People rarely go to jail for crimes in securities frauds. They just resurface in another company again looking for more investors who want to make lots of money.

Sadly, the effect is the same as if a person took your wallet and ran away. You lost the money in the wallet. The only difference is that the wallet thief can be caught, can get convicted and could go to jail while the unethical broker, financial planner or other such person just goes to his next mark for his next take.

This book helps you make money in the investment world in spite of *Thieves on Wall Street*. Knowing a few key rules of the game, how to spot the **get rich quick schemes** and how the industry works can get you an edge.

"It is difficult but not impossible to conduct strictly honest business. What is true is that honesty is incompatible with the amassing of a large fortune quickly."

Mahatma Gandhi

THE BROKERAGE INDUSTRY

The brokerage industry has many faces and functions. You should have a clear understanding of how this industry works and what it can do for you. And **to** you. You can get rich if you use it right and understand its limitations and dangers. If you allow it, you can also go broke and worse yet, be led to bankruptcy, loss of house, family and good health.

The brokerage industry is a vehicle. Like a car that you buy to serve your transportation needs. This car takes you where you want to go. You buy what you need, whether it is a used compact economy car for $5,000 or a Rolls Royce convertible for $300,000. The car you buy sets the tone and style of your transportation. Either way, **you** and only **you** decide where you drive each time you get into it. You are the boss.

The brokerage industry can also be like a big cruise ship where someone else is in charge. The cruise ship owner advertises, calls you and does all kinds of promotions to get you aboard. You receive color brochures of exotic tropical isles, far away places, gorgeous and trim girls and yes, even offers to take you on a gambling trip that can make you rich while you have lots of fun.

Unlike the car where **you** are the captain and in complete charge, you give up your control to the ship's captain. Someone else is in charge of making sure the boat is safe. Someone else is in charge of making sure that the captain is qualified to run it.

You rely on the assumption that the company owning the ship has hired honest people who won't steal your wallet and valuables from your room while you are eating dinner. But, when you get on a ship, you can be exposed to storms, tidal waves, hi-jackings and all sorts of scam artists who may be your dinner tablemates.

When you eat, you hope that the kitchen is clean and the food fresh and doesn't contain salmonella that ruins your stomach for the duration and worse yet, carry you to your grave. When you are on a ship, you give up being in charge of yourself. You trust the owners of the boat and his employees with your life.

When you face the brokerage industry, you have the choice of getting a car where you are the boss or getting on a cruise ship where some one else is in charge. This choice is yours and can be one of the most important decisions of your life. This decision can lead you to riches or rags. It's vital that you understand this and never forget it. Even if you select a car as your vehicle where you are the boss, there are many **ships** along the road beckoning you to stop, get out of your car and into a ship for an adventure. A financial adventure that can make you or ruin your life.

WHAT IS A BROKER?

Broker is a word often used in this book. Let's ask Webster to find out what his dictionary says:

Broker: agent, mediator, intermediary, catalyst, go-between, middleman, negotiator

Karger's Corollary: comers, bringers, wannabees,

    Another definition of broker is: Someone who wants to bring to you something he doesn't have. But wait! How can someone get you anything he doesn't have? Easy. He finds out what you want and how much money you have. Then, he goes to the far corners of the world to find it and brings it to you.

    For this service, the broker gets paid a commission. If the commission is big enough, the broker will do anything to **close** the transaction.

    Aha! Here we have another important word, **closing**. Let's again consult Webster.

closing: Final, completed, decisive, done

Karger's Corollary: You bought it and the money left your bank. You sold it and the money is in your bank.

    The broker serves a very useful function. If you need something you don't have, can't find it or don't want to spend your time and money looking for it, call a broker. On the other hand, if you want to sell something and don't have a ready buyer, call a broker who will look for the buyer. This something can be **anything**. You call the real estate broker if you want a house, warehouse, shopping center or an island and a business broker if you want to buy or sell a business. You need a yacht broker if you are into boats. If you want to hire a body or rent out your wife's, you might need a pimp. Sorry, I almost forgot about stocks, bonds & other financial products. You need stock brokers for these.

Brokers, no matter what kind, have one major thing in common. They find out a lot about you and especially how much money you have and where it is. This is necessary because without knowing a lot about you and what you want and how much you can pay, they can't do the job for you. It gets very personal, as in the case of the pimp.

The reverse of this is the absolute critical need for you to also learn a lot about the broker. It's like getting married to the broker. Or as it is with the pimp, married for the night. Before you tie that knot, it behooves you to spend some time learning about the broker. You could catch empty drafts in your bank account or AIDS, if you engage a pimp.

This brings me to a situation that happened to me. One day, a fellow named Ahmed calls from Houston. He heard that I have good connections in securing a hard to get and large quantity of a Mid-Eastern currency.

He claimed to be closely connected with the King of Saudi Arabia and had worked directly for him. His proposition, if real, would mean millions of Dollars for us both in commissions. I called Nizzar, who really is related to the Royal Family to check out this fellow. Guess what!. Ahmed really did work for the King, as his Royal Pimp. But the King wanted fresh flowers and Ahmed brought home something less than fresh.

So, Ahmed went to the streets to fetch whatever he could for himself and thus, my phone rings. It really pays to spend a little time, sometimes lots of time, before you get to bed with these critters called **brokers**. He could turn out to be one of the *Thieves!*

Now, let's get back to Wall Street and stock brokers. Again, we need to work through a few definitions.

FIRM: The brokerage company like Merrill Lynch. The firm is **Member** of the NASD, NYSE and occasionally other exchanges.

BROKER: The individual person you speak with about stocks and any other investment product. This person must be licensed and registered with the NASD and the state in which the **customer** resides. His title may be Registered Representative, Account Executive, Vice President and may be an employee or independent contractor.

The firm **must** be a member of the NASD and may be a member of a stock exchange like the New York, American, Chicago, etc.

If the firm is not a member of an exchange, it must have an arrangement with a firm that is a member to buy or sell securities traded on that exchange. If the **firm** conducts business in all states, the firm must be **registered** in each of the 50 states and pay fees for this privilege. The firm can be a large public corporation or a one person broker/dealer operating as a **firm.**

Legally, and as far as the NASD, SEC and the states are concerned, the **firm** and the licensed **person** dealing with the public are two separate entities.

The **person**, the Registered Representative or whatever title he has **must** be affiliated with a **member firm**. This person must also be **licensed** to operate as a securities broker by the NASD that administers qualification tests and screens applicants for licenses.

This person must also be individually **registered** in each state where he does business. This registration is separate and apart from the **firm's** registration. The individual broker must pay a registration fee to each state wherein he has clients **and** prospective clients.

The broker is not allowed to even solicit business in a state wherein he is not registered. Moreover, the broker cannot be registered nor do business in any state wherein his firm is not also registered. The dual registration requirement is important because it allows the **state** regulatory agencies to monitor the activities of **firms** and **individuals** and take some action when violations become known.

For an example, if you have a problem with a broker or the broker's FIRM and can't get a satisfactory resolution within a reasonable time, you can call the State regulatory agency and file a complaint against the person, his firm or both. The state has the authority to withdraw the **registration** of the firm and the broker. This means that the state authorities can close down the operations of an entire brokerage firm **within** a state.

WHOSE INTEREST DOES
THE BROKERAGE FIRM SERVE?

The brokerage firm, hereinafter referred to as the **firm**, serves several functions. Some of these are relatively well understood while others may be obscure. It is very important for the investor to know what these functions are because this leads to a better understanding of the broker's role in a specific situation. Does he work for **you**, his client or does his interest and his firm come first?

This is not a question of who gives him his paycheck. Obviously, his paycheck bears the name of his firm. The real question is:

Whose interest does your broker serve?

This is often not clear and yet, it is one of the most important things to know about your broker. Although it is expected that your broker is supposed to serve the best interest of the client, you cannot rely on this assumption. It's much safer to assume that the broker serves someone else's, not yours.

The brokerage industry provides several important functions. It is very important for the investor to clearly understand whose interest is served in specific transactions. The main services and interests served are:

Facilitating the buying and selling of securities between investors, mutual funds, money managers, banks, insurance companies, etc. You, the investor, pay a commission for this service. The brokerage firm and the broker(person) is supposed to serve **your** interest in this transaction.

Providing the means for selling new stock and other securities to the public raising money for Corporations. This is the transfer of ownership from private hands into public hands. This is the process of going public. The firm receives huge fees for this service from the company whose shares are being sold to the public. The interest served here is the firm's and its corporate client.

Assisting Corporations, public and private, in large financial transactions such as acquisitions, mergers, bankruptcies, etc. This is **investment banking**. Again, huge fees are paid to the Firm for these services. Again, the **firm** and its corporate clients are the prime beneficiaries whose interests come **first**.

Creating a market for securities held in the firm's inventory. This specifically means that the Firm has, for a variety of reasons, accumulated securities such as stocks, bonds, warrants, limited partnerships, etc. and is stuck with them. In this case, the interest served is clearly the Firm's.

Research stocks, bonds and other securities. This is done by the Research Department of the Firm and is supposed to give assurance to you, the investor, that the company being recommended by the broker(the person) is financially sound, not overpriced and is an investment consistent with your personal financial situation, goals and best interests. You, the investor pays for this through the commission charged each time you complete a transaction with the Firm.

The interest that is supposed to be served in this case is you, the client. But in reality, this is rarely so. Often, these reports are written to stimulate buying the researched stock(or other security). So that you are motivated to buy, allowing someone else to sell at a higher price. This is part of the distribution phase in the retailing of securities.

The brokerage firm and the individual broker's need to meet sales goals and profit projections. You, the investor might not think this is relevant. To the contrary, this is extremely important because it deals with the self serving interest of the firm and its brokers. You should ask yourself the following question:

Is the broker recommending that you buy a particular stock because of its investment value or does he need to increase his sales and revenues that month to meet his goals and keep his job?

THE BROKER
IS IN THE RETAILING BUSINESS

Let's look up *retailing* in the dictionary to see what the word means. We do this occasionally throughout this book because we often learn important concepts by going back to the basics.

Retailing: Sell, market, barter, distribute,
peddle, vend, promote, hawk,

When the broker calls you and recommends something to you, and often very strongly **encourages** you to say **yes**, you should have a very good understanding of whose interest will be served.

This interest is either yours or the firm's. You should **always, without any doubt,** assume that whatever he is recommending is in **his** best interest. Sure, you could also benefit. But you should accept the reality that your interest is secondary.

He is calling you to generate a commission for himself that day. He needs **your** transaction to earn his daily bread.

If you also make money, the broker will be very happy. Never forget though, that his first and constant concern is to meet his sales quotas, make a very good living for himself and keep his job. Always remember, the broker will make money whether you do or not. That's the system. I mention this often in this book to help you identify one of the *Thieves on Wall Street*.

When the broker calls and recommends something, you better be as sure as you can be that the investment is sound and suitable for you. You must under no circumstances, ever, assume that what the broker tells you is always so. He may believe it, can cite you reports and give you lots of information that supports his statements.

Never, ever forget that he is in the **retailing** business. He needs to make a sale that day to meet his quotas and do whatever it takes to keep his job.

You, the investor, the one who **pays** and takes the **risk**, should always spend some time confirming the broker's information with other totally different and unrelated sources.

You should constantly remember that the broker is a salesman and is retailing a product to you, his customer. He will profit each time you buy or sell. Wait, haven't we covered this ground before? Yes. And we'll continue to visit this subject because it is vitally important.

WHAT DOES THE BROKER
DO FOR YOU?

The stock broker and his firm is where you go to buy and sell stocks, bonds, mutual funds and all sorts of financial instruments. Could you buy and sell these financial things without the broker? Yes, but that wouldn't be practical.

If you wanted to BUY 1000 shares of XYC company, you would have to find out who has these shares available for sale and what price he might be willing to sell them for. Conversely, if you had these shares already but wanted to sell them, you would have to find someone interested in buying them. Whether you are buying or selling, you would have to negotiate the price and terms. That's not all. Let's say you, the seller did get together and agreed on price and terms. Both of you would have to initiate and complete the administrative tasks of recording and handling the transfer of the shares including the banking arrangements. That's a lot of work and requires specialized knowledge. The brokerage firm does all this efficiently using the highly computerized financial system in place today. This system consists of huge capacity central computers, terminals on the desks of most brokers, all of which are interconnected via telephone lines, satellite and radio communications and a host of other high technology systems.

Each brokerage firm and all its branches as well as most desks within each branch are connected to this vast information and computer network. When you talk to a broker, he could be in his office, in his house, car or even on the beach. This is made possible thanks to the marvels of technology.

Let's get back to the 1000 shares of stock XYZ. How would the broker handle this for you?

If you want to buy 1000 shares of XYZ, simply call a broker and he can tell you within seconds the price, volume and all sorts of things about the stock. If you want to sell, he also can tell you, instantly, what the stock is selling for.

You can tell him to sell at the then current market price or specify what price you would be willing to sell at. Later, one minute, an hour or even a month later, when the stock reaches that price, your stock is automatically sold and you receive a confirmation statement in the mail. The payment or receipt funds must be completed within 3 business days of the actual **Trade Date**. This is called **Settlement Date**.

What else can the brokerage firm do for you? Mutual funds, insurance, CD's, bonds, limited partnerships, options, futures and things you cannot even imagine. Yes, the brokerage firm even will issue checks for you to write, give you credit cards and mortgage loans on your real estate.

The firm's goal is to dip into your pockets and bank account to grab all of your money. The modern name for this is **assets under the firm's management.** This is the first step for one of the *Thieves on Wall Street* **to raid your wallet.** Watch out!

HOW DOES THE BROKERAGE FIRM
MAKE MONEY?

When you think about the brokerage firm, think retailing. Think about stores. Go back to the flea market we covered in an earlier chapter. They buy products wholesale and mark it up to retail price. The difference is the store's gross profit. There is a tremendous incentive to price products to the highest level at which you, the customer is willing to pay. The sales people usually get paid commissions for each transaction. The more they sell and the highest price they can get, the more goes into the salesperson's pocket.

Back to the brokerage firm. The firm buys shares of stock of companies that it selects based on popularity, demand and the potential of making a profit. In the case of **NASDAQ** securities, the firm is a **market maker** in this type of transaction. These shares are placed into the firm's inventory. When you call to **buy**, the firm **sells** the shares to you out of its inventory at the price quoted at the time you called. This is the **ask** price. When you call to **sell**, the firm will buy the shares from you at the **bid** price and place it into inventory.

The **ask** price, what you pay, is always higher than the **bid** price, what you receive. The difference is called the **spread** and this is the gross profit to the firm. Let's look at an example. The **bid** for stock XYZ is $10.25 with **ask** at $10.75. The **spread** is the difference which is 50 Cents. If you sold, you would receive $10.25. If you bought, you would pay $10.75. The 50 Cent spread goes to the market maker's pocket who probably gives a piece of it to your broker.

Then, the firm adds a commission to the transaction which increases your cost even more when you buy and reduces what you receive when you sell. This commission is shared between your broker and his firm which adds even more to your broker and his firm's profits.

The brokerage firm however does not have an inventory in all the stocks in the world. That would be impractical, as it would be for a retail store.

When you call to buy a stock and the brokerage firm does not carry it in inventory, the firm will go to other firms that do maintain inventory.

The price you are supposed to pay for this stock is the price the brokerage firm pays plus commission. I say **supposed** because this is rarely the case as the chance is high that the firm will mark it up if you buy and mark it down if you sell.

The only way you could prevent this is to find out exactly what time of the day, hour, minute and second, your stock was bought and the market price at that precise time. The odds are high, that the broker charges **you** the **highest** price the stock sold for that day if you buy and gives you the **lowest** price that day if you sell. In other words, chances are that you will not get the closing price of the day, as reported in the daily stock tables.

Where does the excess profit go? The firm splits it with the broker. This can be substantial, sometimes as much as one Dollar per share or as low as one eighth. On a 1000 share trade, this excess profit can therefore range between $125 and $1000.

You will never see this on your confirmation statement. Can you prevent this? You can try by demanding from the broker a **time and price** sheet listing all transactions in the market on your stock near the time you either bought or sold. The broker and his firm will do everything possible to talk you out of this and delay getting it to you. They don't like it because you got smarter and that dips into the broker's **excess profit** pocket.

The brokerage firms are engaged in other services that generate huge fees. These are investment banking, mergers & acquisitions and bringing private companies public through the IPO (Initial Public Offering).

HOW MUCH MONEY
DO THE BROKERAGE FIRMS MAKE?

Plenty! The profit of the six major brokerage firms is estimated to be about $6 Billion in 1994. Based on an estimated 10% profit margin, this translates to about $60 Billion in revenues. This is just for the six major firms. Assuming this accounts for about 70% of the business, the annual profits would be about $9 billion on $90 billion in revenues. The 1994 financial performance for three selected brokerage firms are given in the following table:

	REVENUE	PROFIT
Merrill Lynch	$18.2	$1.10
Paine Webber	4.0	0.31
Schwab	1.1	0.14

Numbers expressed in Billions of Dollars

The profit stated in the above table is the profit **after** all expenses, including paying the brokers their commissions, the support staff their salaries, the buildings, computers. Everything. Not bad.

When you see these numbers, keep in mind that the brokerage firms make money whether you do or not. Each time you have a transaction or receive a service from the brokerage firm, you are charged. In recent years, some brokerage firms even charge you a fee if you want to transfer your account or take possession of your stock certificates. Some charge annual fees for maintaining IRA accounts. A major source of income is margin interest, the interest **You** pay to the brokerage firms when you have a margin balance.

Look at the commissions paid out to the brokers, the individuals you deal with. These are not included in the above profit numbers. Recent estimates indicate that active and full time brokers average about $125,000 per year in commission income.

There are brokers who make well in excess of a million Dollars while others at small firms make as little as $25,000. The grand daddy of all was Michael Milken, the Junk Bond King who in just one year made about $1 billion.

Do the brokerage firms and their brokers deserve and earn this kind of money? In a free enterprise system, the people and companies making any amount of money deserve what they make so long as it is made legally, ethically and render the service for which they get paid and last, the market is willing to pay it. That service should also be to make **you** money.

How do you get a fair chance in this system? First, you learn how the system really works so that you can make it work for you instead of against you. Second, you shop around for what you really need. Sound familiar? It's like shopping for a car, a boat, a new hi-fi or a pair of shoes. You know what you want and you find out what's available. Then, you take out your wallet and buy it. Just like it is in the retail business. Let's remember an old expression: *Caveat Emptor* - Let the Buyer Beware!

TYPES OF BROKERAGE FIRMS

There are several types of brokerage firms. Each type offers different service levels at varying prices.

Full Service/Full Price: Everything including research, insurance, pension plans, trusts, credit cards and the perceived benefit of talking with persons titled Executive Financial Consultant or Vice President. Examples are Merrill Lynch, Smith Barney, Bear Stearns, etc.

Near Full Service/Discount: Almost everything the full service broker has but at a substantial discount, sometimes as much as 50%. You don't have to pay for a New York office tower and the broker is permitted to negotiate commission rates.

Small Local Broker: Usually a small office financial planner operation and can even be out of the broker's house. Service can be highly personal and include insurance as well as securities. Price is highly negotiable. Commissioned Broker.

Deep Discount Broker: Bare bones brokerage office with only one or just a few offices. Everything is done via toll free 800 telephone. No research, no recommendations, no discussion on the merits of investments. Priced at a deep discount down to as low as $29 per transaction regardless of number of shares or Dollar value or 1.5 Cents per share with a minimum transaction fee of $35. The Broker is a salaried person.

This compares with the full service/full price broker at hundreds of Dollars for the same transaction. The person you speak with is a licensed broker on salary typically making $20-30,000 per year. This type of brokerage firm often also has automated trading and account services available whereby you can use your PC or the touch tone telephone to do your transactions and monitor your account status. In this case, the human broker has been re-engineered out of business.

Computerized Online Brokerage: A brokerage firm offering online computer service that allows you to enter transactions and check your account status using your computer regardless of whether it is from your home, office, car or in a hotel while away on travel. This service is in addition to regular tollfree phone service. When you have questions or problems, you call customer service or send a message via your computer's e-mail system. If you really need to speak with a human, you can always talk with a human who is fully licensed and usually very helpful. Deep discount pricing. Salaried broker.

Penny Stock Broker: Where you get your head handed to you. Principally dealing with very low priced stocks, usually under $1, not on the NASDAQ or the exchanges but on the Electronic Bulletin Board or the Pink Sheets or Canadian stocks trading on the Vancouver Exchange. (See page 57.)

Penny stock brokers typically work in **boiler rooms** usually consisting of a large room divided into small cubicles where brokers sit with head sets. In front of the room there often is a podium where the "Conductor" prompts the brokers in their pitches.

Each broker has a telephone, a head set, a deck of lead sheets or cards and has a quota of making at least 100 calls per day. These are called **cold calls**. This is a **Boiler Room**. The price is very high. A high percentage of customers lose 100% of their entire investment. Brokers are on commission.

Off The Street Broker: Where you deal with unlicensed persons calling themselves consultants. These usually are individuals not connected with any firm and work with situations the brokerage industry avoids. The deals offered by the off street brokers typically are high risk/very high reward and can include currency exchanges, bank notes, financing of high risk projects and even physical commodities like gold, cement and urea. These offerings are typically in the multi-million Dollar level and even on occasion rise to multi-billion Dollar projects.

The persons usually work out of their homes or very small rundown offices with a telephone and a fax and occasionally, a cheap computer. Most of these **off street brokers** have one thing in common. Their telephone bills and rents are usually far behind and they are nearly broke. They are the dream chasers going all the way to the heaven or for broke. Most of them go broke before doing too much damage. Some of them go to jail. A few even get fitted with cement shoes and put to rest at sea.

WHICH TYPE OF BROKER
IS FOR YOU?

Think about the decision whether to rent a car for a trip or book a ship. The car vacation takes you where you want to go, when you want to leave, lets you stay longer where you like it most.

You eat where and when you want and probably the most important thing of all, if you don't like the car, you can go to the nearest car rental office and change it for a different car. Let's not forget, if the weather goes bad, you don't feel well or want to go back home for any reason, you simply turn the car around and go home. No problems, no hassles, no questions. You just do it.

The ship vacation, however, is preset in all respects. You book it far in advance and pluck down serious money. The destination and itinerary are set. You are assigned eating shifts and even a specific table.

May the Lord help you if you want to change the shift, don't like your table mates or ask for a different table. Worse yet, you don't like your room. If you don't like the cruise and want to change to another ship, once it left the dock, you are dreaming. The only recourse you have is to get off at the next port and fly home. You lost thousands of dollars on the uncompleted trip and paid more to fly back home. Worse still, you didn't reach your goal. You didn't have a vacation. You had an expensive nightmare that used up your vacation time and money.

Hold it! This is about picking your broker. Selecting your broker **is** like choosing between a car and a cruise. The car gives you nearly total control while the cruise ship takes it away.

If you want to invest your money without any responsibility, don't care about how much commission the broker charges and are willing to risk losing most of your money, go to the nearest full service brokerage firm and open a **Discretionary Account**.

The manager will introduce you to a broker who will give you forms to sign and ask for your check to open the account. Then, you simply leave and look at the monthly statements that tell you how you are doing.

In this situation, the broker has full authority to do almost anything he wants, within some basic guidelines you agreed on at first. He can buy and sell stocks, bonds, options, warrants, and mutual funds almost at will.

He is the manager of your account and in charge of your money until you yank it away if you are dissatisfied. Hopefully, you will have heard a sharp wake up call before most of it is gone. The discretionary account gives the broker the temptation to trade more often.

You should remember that each trade gives him a commission. This gives him the opportunity to select those products that allow the firm to charge the highest commissions, like mutual funds and options and worse yet, limited partnerships.

The broker doesn't have to call you each time to receive approval on his recommendation. This denies you the chance to know where your money goes and the opportunity to say NO. You pay the highest commission as this is a full service brokerage firm, for the privilege to have a well-dressed broker sitting in a fancy downtown office managing your money. Can you make money at this? Of course. Are you learning anything through this? Probably not. Do you have good control over your money? Definitely not. Could you lose most of your money? Yes. Can you change your mind and get off the **SHIP**?

Yes, but as it was when you took the cruise ship and changed your mind midcourse, it could cost you a bundle. Could the **Discretionary Account** at a full service or any type of brokerage firm expose you to the *Thieves on Wall Street?* Without a doubt.

The brokerage industry offers several different kinds of services:

* Full Service/Full Commission
* Limited Service/Discount
* Deep Discount
* Computerized Online Broker
* Penny Stock/Boiler Room
* Off Street Broker

Let's go to the **Full Service Broker**. This is where you go for everything in financial services. Stocks, bonds, options, partnerships, insurance, credit cards, checking, mortgage loans, personal services and just about anything. Do you need it? Maybe.

If you are starting out and want to learn about investments, a full service brokerage firm might be a good idea. The education might be worth the price of high commissions. After all, if you went to school, you would have to pay for tuition, books and supplies. Spend a great deal of effort selecting the individual broker.

Find someone who is willing to spend a little time with you, give you information and one who won't pressure you into situations that **must be invested in right away or lose the opportunity.** You should never be pressured to rush into anything until you know what you are doing and it feels right. You will always have opportunities.

There will come the time when the broker tells you about a specific situation that does feel right to you. If you feel that you know him well enough, you should not hesitate to go ahead with that opportunity when he calls. Waiting and studying too long on a **buy** or **sell** situations too often will frustrate the broker and cause you to lose out.

If, after a reasonable time, say six months with the broker, he has earned his keep, you might want to stay with him as long as he continues providing a consistent and profitable service. It's the old story, **Don't fix it if it isn't broke.**

Still, you should never stop being informed of your investments and you definitely should continue to check their value in the financial pages of your newspaper or elsewhere. It's **your money** and you should always know what's happening. You worked very hard for it. If you have questions about it, call your broker. He gets paid, through his full service commissions for this service. If he isn't up to date on each of your investments, he isn't doing his job.

If you do use a full service brokerage firm and have a broker with instant access to the world of financial information, still check out the stock yourself. Read the financial press and focus on the industry of the stocks you own and look for news about the companies. Make sure you get on the mailing list for news and reports from the companies you own or those you are considering. This improves your knowledge and serves as a checkpoint on your broker.

If you have a broker you like and are making money with, why should you do all this work? There are many reasons. First, it's like an insurance policy making sure that everything is really going the way you like. Fresh knowledge often prevents surprises that can cost you plenty. It helps you making sure that your broker is keeping up on your account and that your relationship remains fresh and profitable.

If, at some time, you find that you know more than your broker about your situations, you won't need him anymore. You are doing his work while paying him. That's contributing to his income while supporting the billions in profits generated by the full service firms.

Another reason, and a very important one, is that you can instantly take charge of your own account when the broker retires, gets sick, dies or moves to another firm you don't like or worse yet, if his firm goes out of business. You want to be prepared for this because one of these situations will without any doubt happen. Count on it!

Then, you are prepared and can quickly take your money and stocks or whatever else you have to another brokerage firm. Maybe you don't need a full service broker anymore because you already have direct access to information and are familiar with how the business works. Maybe even this book has helped you along gaining this knowledge.

Now, let's go to the **Limited Service/Discount** broker. It's just what the name says. Limited service at a discount. The brokerage firm might offer some services like research reports and cash management accounts. A negative to this type of firm is that usually, the broker is less willing to spend time with you because the commission is less. You may be better off to stay with a full service broker and pay his high commission until you are ready to go to the **Deep Discount Broker**.

When you **are** ready for the **Deep Discount Broker**, you must also be prepared to take total charge and accept full responsibility for your investments and your account. If you are at this stage, you are off the cruise ship and into the car. You now are the captain and in near total control of your financial destiny.

You still receive detailed monthly statements, confirmation of all individual transactions and still can talk to someone at the discount brokerage firm when you have operational questions or problems to resolve. You do your own research, make your own decisions and are in complete charge. You probably by now read much more about investments, subscribe to one or more investment letters or buy specific reports on situations you are interested in.

Your expenses for these have risen since you left the full service broker because he provided some of them at no extra cost. Instead of paying hundreds of dollars, maybe even a thousand or more for a transaction at the full service firm, you now probably spend less than $50 for the same transaction. Your total cost should have dropped dramatically.

If you made the transition from full service brokerage to deep discount broker, learning along the way, you will receive another benefit. This benefit is much more important than the Dollar savings.

You have achieved a high degree of **flexibility**. When you have a stock that hasn't done well and is slightly down from the price you paid, you might have a strong urge to wait until it recovers a little more to break even with the commissions. But if the commissions are very small as they are when you deal with deep discount brokerages, you don't need to wait for that extra 1/8 or 1/4 point rise to cover the commission cost. **One of the most expensive and worst mistakes you can make** is to wait for the stock to recover and consider the commission in that decision.

What happens if the stock doesn't go up that extra fraction and instead goes down one half or two points? You lose and big. This happens more often than not. When it's time to sell a stock, sell it because it is the right decision without any consideration of transaction cost.

The very low transaction cost at the deep discount brokerage makes this decision much easier for you. After a while, you don't even think about commissions. Your entire focus is on **investment decisions, not cost saving decisions**. This alone can make the difference between making lots of money in the markets and losing your wallet to the *Thieves On Wall Street*.

HOW DOES THE MARKET MAKER
GRAB YOUR MONEY?

When you think about **market makers** think about your favorite **flea market**. The stand at the flea market and the person selling at the stand. Look at the following relationships:

Flea Market: The NASDAQ System
Stand: Market Maker
Person: The Trader

You probably have heard about these critters and how they rape the investors with their wide spreads. We have visited them already in this book.

Who are they? How do they work? How can they extract excess profit from a trade at your expense?

A *market maker* is a brokerage firm that is a member of the NASD, the National Association of Securities Dealers. Besides acting as a **broker** who facilitates buying and selling between clients, this brokerage firm also buys and sells for its own account. This is the **market making** function with the work assigned to the firm's trader.

The firm buys from you at the **bid** and **sells** to you at the **ask** which is also known as the **offer** price. The difference is the **spread** which is the market maker's profit. Look at it this way. The market maker buys the stock at wholesale and sells to you retail at the marked up **ask** price.

The mark up is intended to compensate the market maker for his risk and expenses, just like the guy at the flea market. Unlike the flea market where you can shop prices and see what you get, you, the clients have almost no such opportunity with the market maker.

The trader can mark it up almost at will to the highest level the market will allow. You can bet that the market-maker and his trader will take full **advantage** of your **disadvantage**.

Let's move to commissions charged by the market maker. But wait! He isn't supposed to charge commissions because the broker told you that his firm will sell you **net** at the **ask** and buy from you **net** at the **bid**. So how can we talk about commissions when we deal with market makers?

Easy. Did you notice that when you sold the stock, the **bid** was $10 1/4 but you received only $10 1/8? You called the broker and asked why you only received $10 1/8? He gave you some double talk about the stock trading up and down during the day and your trade executed at the time the stock was $10 1/8.

You shrug it off. After all, you made a little money on the stock and the stock does move up and down a little during the day.

Then, you remember that when you bought the stock, you were charged 1/8 above the **ask** and were told the same thing. What's happening here?

I analyzed transactions at a brokerage firm over a one year period. Guess what I found?

Never once did a **sell** transaction execute above the lowest closing **bid** for the day and conversely, never once did **buy** transaction execute below the closing **ask**. Following a thorough analysis of all transactions, I learned that the broker had an arrangement with the market maker's **trader**. He always added for himself an eight or a quarter a point and included it in the **net** to the client with zero commission showing on the statement. This **markup** on the **buy** side and **markdown** on the **sell** side usually exceeded the commission if that had been disclosed as a separate item on the confirmation statement.

What really happened here is that the brokerage firm making market in the stock created an arrangement between the broker and the trader whereby the broker set the **net** to the client covering his commission with the rest being split between the trader and the firm.

This agreement allows the firm to keep 100% of the spread thus eliminating the need to give the broker a portion of that spread for his commission. This is a **hidden commission**.

Doesn't this system encourage the highest possible spread and cooperation between market makers to keep the spreads as wide as possible? It sure does. And it is at **your** expense. This practice is at the root of the Justice Department 1995 investigation alleging price fixing by the NASD and its market making members.

Not all broker dealers are market makers nor are all market makers required to make a market in all stocks. The firm can pick and choose which stocks to make a market in and can start and stop almost anytime. Just like at the flea market. The vendor comes and goes depending on the opportunities he sees and charges whatever the market allows.

Let's now look at how the system works and what happens inside the brokerage firm. This will help you understand what's going on when you deal with these critters.

The brokerage firm making market in designated stocks assigns a person to handle this task. This person is called the *trader* who acts on the instructions of the firm's owner or a very senior manager. A firm may have one or many traders depending on how big it is and how many stocks it handles as a market maker.

The trader's workstation is a computer terminal usually called the QUOTRON that is part of the NASDAQ system. NASDAQ stands for the National Association of Securities Dealers Automated Quotation System. Typically, each trader has his own QUOTRON terminal.

The QUOTRON is connected through dedicated lines to the NASDAQ central computer located in Virginia and through it, a vast telecommunications network interconnecting all NASD broker dealers, many of which are market makers. A firm wanting to make market in stocks must subscribe to the highest level of service offered by the NASD.

This allows the firm to post **bid** and **ask** prices on the computer screens available to all NASD members. Here is what happens.

The trader is instructed by his firm to initiate making a market for stock XYZ. The QUOTRON displays 12 other firms also making a market in XYZ at various prices. The trader, following guidelines given by his management then posts his **bid** and **ask** prices, which become visible to all market makers on the NASDAQ system.

If a market maker somewhere on the system **bids** to buy 100 shares at $5 and that's the **ask** of a market maker just placing 100 shares for sale, there is a match and the shares are bought at $5. The market maker who bought the 100 shares at $5 then sells the 100 shares to the retail client at the **ask** which is $5 1/2. The market maker's profit or markup is 50 Cents. If the retail client wants to **sell** 100 shares, the market maker will buy the shares at that **bid** of $5 and then offer them for sale at the **ask** price on the QUOTRON to the entire NASDAQ network. Again, this market maker makes 50 Cents on the markup.

The trader working on behalf of the market maker is typically paid a salary because he acts as an employee of the firm and does not normally interface with retail clients. Additionally, he is paid an incentive to trade in such a manner that results in the greatest profit to the firm. The bigger the profit, the bigger the bonus.

This means that he will do everything and anything he can, within the rules to strike a profitable balance between volume and spreads. He also has an incentive to make special deals with the brokers. The more creative the trader is, the more of the client's money is kept inside the firm and shared between broker, trader and the firm. Unfortunately, all of this is at **odds with the client's best interest.** Under the right circumstances, the market maker and his trader could become:

Thieves on Wall Street

WHEN THE PENNY STOCK BROKER CALLS

Hang up!

But how will you know it is a **penny stock broker** calling? Unless your ears and brain are trained to know, it is very hard. Unfortunately, some learn too late. After this *Thief on Wall Street* has already paid his visit and raided your bank account.

Let's get you ready for that call. First, we need to define **penny stock broker**: A broker strongly touting stocks that typically trade at pennies per share. Less than a Dollar.

Usually, you will find these stocks priced between 3 and 50 Cents. Occasionally, they rise above one Dollar but not by much.

The person calling will be someone you don't know. He will introduce himself as Steve Gold, Account Executive of an investment banking firm. The first thing he will do is ask you if you are interested in an opportunity to make a lot of money. *"Yes, of course"*, you answer. Who wouldn't be interested in making money? The second statement you will probably hear is about the wonderful profits his firm has made for its clients in several recent situations. Next, he will tell you about this absolutely great situation that has **just** come up. A situation ready to make a major move. He tells you something about a new contract, a new cure for **AIDS** or an imminent takeover.

If you act now, you could get in on the **ground floor** and buy 10,000 shares for just 30 Cents per share. Since his firm **makes a market** in the stock, a lucky coincidence, you don't have to pay any commission. A great opportunity. How can anyone say no to a proposition that suggests you could double your money?

You ask one or two basic questions. Like how much revenue is the company doing? Is it making a profit? At that instant, visualize what his face is like. He has a broad smile and points his hand up for his **boiler room** manager to see. You have been **hooked**. You listened to him for just one minute and you asked a question. This was the first **close**. That is, closing in on your bank account.

Then, the caller, yes he is a stock broker although you may yet not realize that, asks if he could send you a package of information on this wonderful situation. "Of course", you reply. What do you have to lose? Plenty, except you don't realize this yet.

He proceeds to verify your address, the best time to reach you and maybe even asks what you do for a living. Just enough to get you to gain just a little familiarity with him, leading to **trust** later on.

One or two days later, you receive either a Federal Express or Priority Mail envelope with some information on a company vaguely described during the telephone call, a list of stocks bought and sold by the investment banking firm and how much was made on each situation. Most of these stocks doubled and even tripled. Included also is an account application with a sheet instructing you how to wire transfer funds directly from your bank account to the brokerage firm's bank.

If this is what happened to you, or something even remotely like it, the best thing you can and should do is to throw the package away. Then, when the phone rings the day after, and it will, you tell the broker you are definitely not interested. If he persists by asking if you don't want to make money and get rich, just hang up.

If you do this, you could have prevented one of the serious mistakes made by many people which led to losing most of their life's savings and even worse yet, money they borrowed to invest with.

Wait a minute. This can't happen. Didn't the government put these penny stock brokers out of business? The guy who called has to be legitimate or he wouldn't be calling. Right?

Wrong! Sure, the government did put the big penny stock brokers out of business. In fact one or two of the more famous ones may still be in jail. But for each big firm closed down, there are several smaller firms still around and pop up as soon as one is closed down. It's like trying to keep balloons stay below the water. They often call themselves **investment boutiques, broker dealers or investment consultants**. But their product is the same as it always was. Penny stocks and products designed to generate huge commissions and profits for the brokers.

Let's look at their investment ideas and how the system works. Can you make money? Yes indeed and lots of it. Can you make money at the crap tables or at the lottery? Yes and lots of it. Are the rewards worth the risk? Only you know that. This book brings you the **inside story** on how the system works. **You** decide how to use it.

WHAT IS A BOILER ROOM?

When the penny stock broker calls, you should visualize his office. This helps you get a perspective of the product being offered and leading you to the right decision.

Let's visit the office. Typically, this is also called a boiler room. How do I know what a boiler room looks like and how it operates? I worked in one for about two months as a broker.

I sat in a very small cubicle with a board for a desk, just big enough for a telephone, rolodex, writing pad and a deck of lead cards. This cubicle was one of about 50 in a large open room. The cubicles were separated by a temporary wall board up to shoulder height and then glass to head height. A platform with a podium and a high stool was at the front of the room.

Each cubicle's telephone was connected to this podium so that all brokers could be monitored and on occasion, the director could intervene to **assist** when he decided it was necessary. The director acted like the **conductor** of an orchestra. There were times when he would flash a light on my desk which signaled me to listen to his prompts. These prompts could be anything from verbal, waving hands or sharp expletives if I wavered too far from the script. The prompts were intended to coach me in whatever I was saying on the phone to the prospect.

Everything was preplanned and rehearsed. The first call. The follow-up call. Sending out the package. Money wiring instructions. When to turn the prospect over to the sales director.

Everything was designed to set the stage for the second call to the prospect. The second call is crucial to the broker because this is equivalent to the vacuum cleaner salesman getting the front door and plugging in his demonstration machine to clean the carpet. But in this case, the penny stock broker can *vacuum* your money right out of your bank account.

That's the time when the pressure will be put on the prospect, if he will answer and give even a hint of interest. Hear now the words of penny stock brokers and brokers in general making cold calls.

"Invest **now**. Do it **today**. The ship is leaving the dock. Don't get left behind. The train is leaving the station. Are you aboard? Will you be left behind? Are you ready to see your money doubling and maybe quadrupling within the next few months? Aren't you interested in making money? What stands in the way for going ahead today? Can I fax you additional information? You are in luck. Our Director of Research just came in. Let me put him on the phone with us to talk more about this company and its prospects."

Is this the type of operation you want to do business with? Only **you** can answer that one.

WHAT ARE PINK SHEETS
AND
PENNY STOCKS?

Penny stocks are stocks typically priced below one Dollar, often right down to just a few pennies. Yes, even as low as one Cent. You should be aware though, that some people consider stocks below $5 as penny stocks even though a few might even be listed on the New York Stock Exchange and represent respectable corporations.

Could you find penny stocks listed in your local newspaper, the Wall Street Journal or any easily available publication? Probably not. Why don't the papers list them so you can easily track the prices? Because they aren't on the NASDAQ or any listed exchange. But you will find them in the **Pink Sheets** or on the **Electronic Bulletin Board**.

Are the pink sheets the fresh linen on your bed ready for you and your favorite friend? No. The Pink Sheets of the securities industry is a listing of **bid** and **ask** prices for thousands of stocks printed on pink and very thin tissue paper normally issued weekly. The BID and ASK prices are not the real prices at which you would buy and sell. Rather, these are representative prices reflecting a survey of the market makers in the given stocks and not the price you would get on a particular day.

These are the stocks that, for a variety of reasons, don't qualify for listing on the NASDAQ or the exchanges. You should also be aware that stocks on these listings also include companies that fell below the minimum requirements to remain on the NASDAQ or the exchanges.

These reasons could include loss of much or even all operating revenue, continued losses exceeding capital assets, significant contingent legal liabilities and maybe just a significant loss of financial health. All of which could be a very big negative from an investment value standpoint.

Pink Sheet stocks rarely reach the NASDAQ and very few make it big. Here, you will find marginal mining and oil companies and development stage companies with no revenues. You could find companies representing no more than a promotion or what's left of a company after bankruptcy liquidation.

Often, promoters issue stock through an investment banker specializing in penny stocks. Management simply puts together a great looking business plan and makes a deal with the investment banker who sells lots of shares, maybe 20 million or more to you for 20 Cents per share.

This raises about $4 million with the firm possibly receiving only $3 million with the rest going to the investment banker and the brokers. The $3 million going to the company is probably split so that the founders personally receive $1.5 million with the rest going for operations and salaries for themselves. Not a bad showing for a few entrepreneurs.

Typically, the investment banker also receives additional shares and warrants that he can later convert into cash by selling even more shares to you. These are the shares you are encouraged to buy when the *penny stock broker* calls.

Pink Sheet companies typically have:

* Little or no revenue
* No profits and big losses
* Lots of shares, often over 100 million
* Little operating capital
* Few employees, often only one or two.

Let's go to the **Electronic Bulletin Board**. This is nothing more than a list of selected **Pink sheet** companies **bid** and **ask** prices placed on an electronic bulletin board operated by the NASD.

These stocks do not qualify for NASD listing although generally, they are somewhat better quality situations than those still on the pink tissue paper. Importantly, the market makers can post the **BID** and **ASK** prices on this board electronically thus making quotes available daily, rather than having to wait for the physical distribution of the hard copy **Pink Sheet** listings.

These are also accessible through several electronic quote services available to the brokers and the general public.

Are these the companies you would want to invest your hard earned Dollar in? You should be very careful when you crawl into a bed of pink sheets cavorting with your favorite penny stock broker.

As in **Ali Baba and the Thieves of Babylon**, the penny stock broker hawks at your wallet:

Open Sesame, Open Sesame

HOW DOES THE PENNY STOCK
SYSTEM WORK?

Now that we have a basic understanding of penny stocks, penny stock brokers, boiler rooms and pink sheets, let's see how all this works together. This system has evolved for many years and was made famous by a well known Denver based penny stock firm and a New Jersey firm whose president advertised his stocks from a helicopter on TV ads.

This system is still very much alive despite us being told that the SEC and state regulators have put it away. While the regulators have done some good in this area, the phone still rings from brokers working in boiler rooms.

Some of these calls are from brokers having been trained in the penny stock environment and now work from nice offices in major brokerage houses. The technique is the same and the results can be just as disastrous.

Let's go back to the time the broker called with that great deal for you. When he told you that you could so easily **double** and even **triple** your money in no time at all. The deal you couldn't pass up. The gravy train you simply couldn't afford to miss.

"Mr. Mark, let me tell you about one of our recent situations. We recommended stock ABC when it was just 20 Cents only two months ago and as we speak, it's already up to 40 Cents."

"Where, Mr. Mark, could you double your money in this short time? Let me tell you about our new situation that right now is at 20 Cents. We just heard that the company is expected to announce a major new contract."

Let's take a close look at this profound statement to understand what it really means. Yes, the stock mentioned by the broker was 20 Cents when he called. But did the shares double?

Probably not. In fact, chances are very good that you would have made no money at all if you had bought that stock.

The broker and his firm made lots of money, though. Here is what happened. Read closely. If you understand this example, you will know how the system works and be ready for that next *Thief on Wall Street* when he calls.

First, let's remember the difference between the **bid** and **ask** prices in stock quotations. You pay the **ask** price when you buy and receive the **bid** price when you sell(ignoring commission costs for the simplicity). The difference goes to the broker and his firm. When the broker said that the price two months ago was 20 Cents, he probably gave you the **bid**, the price you would have received if you sold at that time. That was the **real value**. What he probably didn't tell you was that the **ask** was 30 Cents, the price you had to pay if you bought. That would have been your **real cost**.

Was the price really 40 Cents when he called? Probably. But what he didn't tell you was that the **bid** at that time was 30 Cents, the very price you would have paid, had you actually bought that stock he mentioned. If you had bought two months ago at 30 Cents(the **ask** price) and sold today at 30 Cents, the current **bid**, your profit would have been exactly **zero**. Since there probably was a commission at least on the **sell** side, you actually would have lost money.

How much did the broker and his firm make? Penny stocks typically sell in the thousands of shares at any given time and the smallest transaction probably is 10,000 shares. At first glance, the broker made $1000 profit. This is the difference between the **bid** and **ask**. Do you remember how the market maker works? He made $1200 by adding 2 Cents per share commission on the sell side.

Now, let's take a second look at this transaction to see what the broker really made. You bought the 10,000 shares at 30 Cents for a cost of $3,000. The spread was 10 Cents which is conservative because the spread for penny stocks typically would have been 20 Cents, not the 10 Cents given in this example. So far, the broker made $1000. What would you have made? If the **bid** rose to 30 Cents, you made no money at all. Rather, you would have lost if you subtracted the commission. What kind of a deal is that?

Did the broker just make $1,000? Probably not. The chances are that he made much, **much more.** To estimate what he could have and probably made, we go back to the time when the penny stock broker called and introduced himself as an investment banker.

Let's again review what an **investment banker** does. He brings new shares to the market in the process of raising money for the public company. The broker calling you probably works for the investment banking/brokerage firm that brought the company(stock) public.

The fees paid to the investment banker typically consists of cash and some of the shares issued. In this case, let's assume that 20 million shares were issued and that the investment banker was issued 1 million shares as part of his fee, adding to the $500,000 cash fee already received. The chances are that the shares you bought are part of the free shares thus giving a $3,000 profit to the broker, rather than the $1000 calculated based on being a market maker. In this case the broker acts as a principal, selling from stock received **free** from the company.

Could you have lost the entire $3,000? You bet and real easy. Many of the penny stock companies, as mentioned previously, have no revenues and less than adequate financial resources to accomplish what their business plan calls for. After the initial push by the investment banker is over and he has sold all the inventory shares, there is a good chance for the market to dry up for the shares you just bought.

This means that if you want to sell, there aren't many buyers around and you could be selling out for a mere pennies just to cover the commission.

We have spent extra time with the penny stock situations because it is an area where many investors still get burnt. The *Survival Guide For The Investor* in this book gives suggestions on how to deal with penny stocks, the people who promote them and stocks in general.

Before closing this section, let's remember that low price stocks can occasionally be offered by large and well known brokerage firms. Yes, the management of these firms encourage their brokers to use the rolodex and make cold calls. Cold calls means that the broker is calling strangers from a list provided by his firm or purchased even by himself from list services.

Let's look at a real example of a situation I personally handled that involved one of the most respected brokerage firms on Wall Street. A client told me that his broker, from the large firm had strongly urged him to buy at least 10,000 shares of a stock priced at $2.5.

He asked that I confirm that it indeed was a sound investment through our independent research. We learned the following about the company recommended by the brokerage firm:

* No meaningful assets
* A negative net worth
* A need to issue new shares to
  raise capital for operations
* Consistent and increasing losses

We kept asking ourselves **why** a large brokerage firm would even get involved with this sort of thing and we pressed further in our investigation. The answer was found in a footnote in one of many filings to the SEC. The brokerage firm had at one point provided investment banking services to the company and received stock as part of the fee arrangements.

The brokerage firm was suddenly anxious to sell these securities at the best possible price, as quickly as possible.

The brokerage firm made a market in the securities to facilitate the sale. In other words, the brokerage firm had an inventory it wanted to get rid of before the stock collapsed. Who was available to buy the stock? Clients of the brokerage firm, of course. Luckily, one of those was also our client.

I advised our client that the investment offered was bad and should be totally avoided because it had a good chance to go to zero in a short time. He followed my advise.

Within three months, the stock had been delisted from NASDAQ and fallen into the **pink sheets** to 5 Cents. The stock became worthless in another 3 months as there had begun a criminal investigation into a possible fraud and the company was liquidated. Had my client taken the advise of his broker, he would have lost $25,000 plus commission. But, the broker would made his commission and his firm would have sold its inventory shares at a huge profit, since it received these shares free in exchange for services provided.

We have focused into these situations with great detail to examine the **process**. We have done this even at the risk of being repetitive analyzing how the system works, from an inside point. By understanding the process and how the system really works, you can be better prepared to meet another *Thief on Wall Street.*

WHOSE INTEREST DOES THE RESEARCH DEPARTMENT SERVE?

Your broker called telling you that his firm's research department just a few minutes ago issued a **strong buy** on stock XYC. He also told you that you better hurry to get some of this stock or you'll miss out on a great opportunity.

What does all this mean? Let's go inside Wall Street again to learn more about **how the system really works.**

The full service brokerage firm typically has three main divisions:

Investment Banking: Raises money for companies
Research Department: Evaluates the companies
Retail Division: Buys and sells stocks for clients

I focus on these because they are structured for one common purpose. Making money for the firm. The investment banking department receives fees from the companies for which money is raised. The retail department gets commissions and spreads from you, the client, when you buy and sell.

The research department, staffed with very highly paid analysts equipped with the latest computers costs a lot of money. Who pays for all this? You do, through the commission and often, the company being written up pays. Wait a minute. That can't be. How can a company being recommended be allowed to pay for the research? Isn't that a clear conflict of interest? Yes, and the system gets around this by allowing the brokerage firm to get paid indirectly from the companies recommended.

Let's again open Wall Street's door and go inside for the answers. Why do you suppose that brokerage firms issues research reports on **some** companies and not others? Does the firm select only companies with solid financial fundamentals and great promise?

Knowing these answers and clearly understanding them will give you insight into Wall Street few gain in a lifetime. The answers are not the ones you might expect.

Brokerage firms issue research reports for three main reasons.

FIRST, it gives the broker a sales tool. If the broker tells you to buy the stock because he says it's a good investment, you might think about it. But if the broker tells you that his Vice President and Managing Director of Research has issued a **buy** recommendation, would you be better motivated to act **today**?

SECOND, it gives the brokerage firm the means of selling inventory shares acquired as part of the fee received for providing investment banking services for corporate clients.

THIRD, it gives the brokerage firm a means of boosting shares of client companies with which it has an investment banking relationship while creating an incentive for new potential clients to sign up.

Have you ever noticed or even thought about why it is that large firms rarely issue research reports on small and medium sized companies **unless** these firms purchase investment banking services from the firm? Have you ever noticed that brokerage firms often provide investment banking services to companies in serious financial trouble, bankruptcy proceedings, restructuring or mergers?

The next time your broker tells you to buy a stock because his firm has issued a research report, **Always** ask him if his firm has an investment banking or other relationship with the company written up. Securities regulations require him to make this disclosure and it is supposed to be in the fine print somewhere, usually at the end of the research report. Where no one sees it. Most people don't even know to ask about it. Now **you** do.

You should already know the answer to this question:

Is the broker recommending the stock because of its excellent value or because the firm has inventory stock to sell or a need to raise money for his firm's corporate client?

The bottom line of this is to give you the chance to figure out if the broker is telling you to buy for **your own good** or **his firm's good**.

Let's move on to another dimension of the research department. Have you ever noticed that stocks often rise **before** the broker tells you about the new research report and then declines after the report is **issued?** Should it not be the other way?

Yes, it should but it usually doesn't happen that way. Why? You are the retail buyer. By the time it reaches you, it has passed though other hands. Mutual funds, money managers, institutional investors and traders. Each time the stock changed hands, it was marked up by market makers or the exchange specialist and commissions were charged along the way. In other words, it went through the entire chain of distribution through wholesale and now, you the retail person bought it.

You will see the stock rise after you bought it **only** if someone else believes it's worth more than you paid. Who will that be? Will you make the calls to stimulate this new demand? Will you write the research reports that can accomplish this task?

Now, after you bought the stock, you see it drift slowly down. But you don't worry. The broker tells you this is only temporary and you are in for the long pull.

Six months later, the stock has lost 30% of its value and you start worrying. The market is sloppy. The stock gurus talk about a bear market. The interest rates are rising. You worry more.

One day, the market drops 75 points and it gets on the front page of your paper. That day you call the broker and **sell**. You want to preserve your cash. Your retirement and savings. You throw in the towel. You are out!

The next day, the market calms down. A few weeks later you notice that your stock is up a little. You start sweating. Did you sell out at the low? Did you screw up? Who bought your stock?

The institutions, mutual funds, money managers and a few savvy individual investors who understand how the markets behave and how the system works. The very ones who had sold it to you six months ago. The stock had dropped to wholesale value again and the wholesalers bought it up for later sale at a higher retail price. Could it be that we again encountered *Thieves on Wall Street?*

Will you be ready for them the next time?

"It is fatal to enter any war without the knowledge and will to win it".

Douglas MacArthur

HOW CAN A MARGIN ACCOUNT
MAKE OR BREAK YOU?

Let's define the word **margin**: Excess, stretch, edge, fringe, brink, beyond, border, outskirt, side.

Do these words suggest that you should enter a margin with some caution? You bet!

If you swim beyond the safety of lifeguard coverage on the beach, you are beyond the **margin** of safety. If you take your car to 100 MPH on any road, you are going beyond the **margin** of safety of the car and the road.

If you stretch your tolerance in running the marathon, you test the limit or **margin** of your body's capacity to remain alive. If you stretch your credit beyond your means, you risk going bankrupt if you lose your job or face other serious loss of income.

Margin is associated with adventure, greed or just simply the need to do better than your ordinary means allow. You can use your resources available **at the margin** to stretch yourself beyond your means. If you are an athlete and want to do more than your body's capacity allows, you get steroids to **temporarily** increase that capacity.

If you are in business and want to grow but don't have the cash on hand you need, you borrow the rest. If you are an individual and want to buy more stock than your cash allows, you borrow the rest from the broker. This is called a **margin account**.

Margin can be very good to you, just like it can be when you borrow to expand your business and increased revenues roll in as a result. **Margin** can also be bad and ruin you if you borrow to expand the business and the revenues don't follow. Just as it can be disastrous if you borrow money from your broker to buy more stock and the stock goes **down** too much.

Buying stock on margin from your broker can also be very **good** for your **broker.** The transaction is bigger which gives him a higher commission.

His firm also benefits because it receives **interest** from you. After all, you borrowed the money, just like you would have at the bank. And, just like at the bank, the brokerage firm borrows its money at a rate lower than you pay. This gives the firm a profit, beyond what it receives from commissions, market making and other charges you pay already. Trading on margin also leads to more frequent transactions which gives the broker and his firm even more commission income from you.

How can a margin account work for and against you? What are the mechanics of a margin account? Knowing this can make you a lot of money but also expose you to added financial risk. It's critical that you understand the system so you know how to manage that risk while still taking advantage of the opportunities a margin account can offer.

Let's see how a margin account works by going through an example. How you can make lots of money and how you can lose your shirt.

Sharp, your broker calls and tells you that stock XYZ is about to make a big move **up**.

"Mr Mark, you should get some and right away, before it's too late."

"Wish I could, Sharp, but I don't have any money right now. I'll have to let it go this time."

"No problem", says Sharp, the broker, who needs to get this **sale** in to meet his **sales quota** before the month closes out.

"Mr. Mark, I have great news for you", Sharp continues. "You really do have the money. Here is how you can buy 1000 shares without sending in even one Cent."

You have several stocks in the account worth $20,000. This means that you can borrow $10,000 cash or buy twice that amount in marginable stock.

Stock XYZ is at $10 which means that you can buy 2,000 shares on **margin**. If you did, you would owe the brokerage firm $20,000 and have stocks totaling $40,000. This would put you at 50% margin, which is the maximum you could get, at the time of purchase.

It's simple, the brokerage firm lends you the money, keeping **all** your stocks as collateral. The margin agreement you signed allows the broker to sell your stocks if the stock price falls below certain minimum maintenance levels **unless** of course you send the broker more money, should that ever happen. That's called a **margin call**.

"Sharp, I don't feel right about doing this. What if the stock doesn't go up or worse yet, if any of the stocks go down? I would have to keep paying interest and worse yet, I might have to send in more money if I should get a margin call."

"Don't worry" Sharp replies, "this stock is really going to fly. When it goes to $20, you can sell it, having doubled your money. Then, you put $40,000 into your account, paying off the whole margin loan and put $20,000 cash in your pocket. Money you can use for anything. A vacation, a new car or even buying more stocks."

"Ok, Sharp, go ahead. You say this is a good investment. How can I lose?"

At dinner that night, your wife sees a new look on your face. "Sweetie, what's happening?"

"Honey, do I have great news for you. Our broker, Sharp, called today with this stock that looks really good. It's supposed to go to $20 and is just $10 now. We bought 2,000 shares. We'll make $20,000 profit!"

"How, Sweetie, can we buy $20,000 in stock when we don't have any money and are scraping to save up for getting the house painted?"

"Don't worry about a thing. We had margin reserves in the account and don't have to send in even one penny. Boy, do we have a smart broker. I'm sure glad we found him."

The next morning, you rush out to get your paper. Instead of going right to the sports page, you hurry to the stock tables in the business section. The stock you bought closed yesterday at $9 3/4. That can't be. You just paid $10 for it yesterday. You call Sharp right away. "Sharp, how come is the stock down from what I paid, just yesterday?"

"No problem, the stock closed on the **bid**, which was $9 3/4. You paid $10 which was the **ask** price at the time we bought yesterday."

A week later, you see the stock drop to $9 and again call the broker. "Hey Sharp, why is the stock down? I have lost $2,000 in just one week. Doesn't this mean that I am below 50% in the margin account?"

"Don't worry, it's just a temporary situation. Stocks will fluctuate. In fact, a few of my other clients are buying more since it's even a better deal at $9."

Three weeks later, you wake up to a headline in the paper:

STOCKS CRASH 100 POINTS ON RISING INTEREST RATES

You go right to the stock tables and look up your stocks. You are horrified. Your chest starts pounding. Stock XYZ dropped to $7. But that's not all. Your other stocks dropped also. You make a quick calculation and really start sweating. The total value in your account has dropped to only $30,000. That's a $10,000 loss! Your equity is now only 33%. And the minimum equity required is 35%.

You start to shake. "What will I do now? I'll get a **margin call**. Where will I get the money to pay it?"

Just as you get to your office, the phone rings. It's Sharp, the broker.

"I guess you saw the paper this morning. We are in a temporary market correction. Please remember, it's just temporary and it will recover."

"Oh yes" Sharp continues, "we do have a problem with the account. Since the stocks dropped, it created a **margin call** and we are required to receive $12,000 cash within 5 business days to cover it. But don't worry, if the stocks go up before the 5 days are up, the margin call is either canceled or reduced, depending on how much we recover. But if you have the money, it would be a real good idea to send it in right away."

"Just in case the market takes a little longer to recover or in case it goes a little lower. Could you give us a check today?"

"Sharp, hell no! I told you that we didn't have the money to buy that stock and you said to use the margin reserves. I didn't have the money then and don't have it today."

"Well then", Sharp replied, we'll just have to hope the stocks go up. But don't worry. Chances are good that will happen. In any case, I'll call you if we have to sell some of the stocks we now have, to cover the margin."

You got no work done that day, calling the brokerage office every hour and listening for the business news on the radio. The news wasn't good. The market was still dropping and your stock now was down to $6.

That night was bad. No sleep. Headache and nausea. Your wife thinks you have the flu because you haven't told her a thing. You don't dare! The phone rings when you get to the office. It's Sharp, the broker.

"Mr. Mark, I got bad news. We went below 30% equity at yesterday's close. My boss says we have to get the $12,000 right away, like this morning."

"But Sharp, I told you, we don't have that kind of money laying around. What can we do?" "Well, Sharp says, I guess I'll have to tell the trader to sell enough stock to cover the **margin call**. We don't have any choice in this."

"I wish we could wait for the market to rebound. But we are bound by SEC rules, house rules and Federal Reserve margin requirements. We have to start selling right away, just in case the market goes even lower, Sharp concluded."

The phone rings about 2:00 in the afternoon. It's Sharp, the broker again. "We had to sell the whole account to cover the margin call, because it was more than $12,000 since the stocks were even lower than yesterday. The total value of all your stocks was $27,000. After paying the $20,000 loan, the accumulated interest and commissions, we have $6,000 left."

"Wait a minute Sharp, did you say we sold **all** my stocks, not just the one you insisted me getting just a few weeks ago? The one which was supposed to double?"

"I am afraid so" Sharp replies. "I'm sorry. This came on us so suddenly and unexpectedly. But we really can't be held responsible for market conditions. That's totally out of our control."

"Sharp, do you mean that all we have left is $6,000? Is that **all** we have left? Why that means we have lost $14,000 in less than a month. And now, we don't even have the original stocks left either?"

"I'm sorry" Sharp replied. "But not to worry too much. We can use the $6,000 to get in a lower price stock where we can make up for the loss in no time at all. I'll call you next week with some **fresh** ideas."

"Like hell you will, Sharp. Don't you ever call me again! Not only has your bird brained idea of going all the way on margin cost us almost all our savings, I now have to face my wife and kids with this and how we can deal with this $14,000 sudden loss."

Three months later, you dare look again in the stock tables for your stocks. You squint your eyes trying not to really see what you fear the most. That the stocks are back up again. A pain in the chest. Your eyes get moist. Your own stocks, the ones you had before getting sucked in by Sharp, were right back to what they were and in fact up a little. That dog Sharp had put you in was even lower.

Let's close up this section on **margin** by reviewing what really happened. The broker made extra commissions by selling you the 2,000 shares, so he could meet his monthly sales goal, the brokerage company received interest from the margin loan. And yes, Sharp, the broker made extra commissions when he forced you to sell all your stocks in that disastrous margin call. Everybody made money except you, who lost a whopping $14,000 and now face divorce because your wife threw you out.

What happened isn't too different than not paying the mortgage on your house. The bank has the right to foreclose on your house if you don't make payments. Foreclosure means that the bank takes possession of your house which is the collateral to your mortgage loan, evicts you from your home, sells the house and pockets the money. If you are lucky, you get the difference between the sale price and the amount you owed plus the expenses the bank had in evicting you and selling your house. There usually isn't anything left. The lawyers make sure about that.

The use of a **margin** stock account can be very profitable. But you must know how the system works and completely understand its risks. If you don't, it's like inviting another *Thief on Wall Street* into your life.

"A small debt produces a debtor; a large one, an enemy."
Pubillius Syrus

BEWARE OF
DISCRETIONARY ACCOUNTS

Discretionary accounts are dangerous and should be avoided. I will say this right up front, so there will be no possibility of missing this statement. **Never open a discretionary account with a broker.**

What is a discretionary account? You establish a **discretionary account** when you give your broker the authorization to make all decisions on your behalf. You sign an agreement whereby he can buy and sell almost any security(stocks, options, bonds) without **first** telling you and receiving your approval. The broker is supposed to invest your money based on certain guidelines agreed to between you and the broker.

Putting it in another way, you give the broker the freedom to buy and sell your stocks based on **his** best judgment. Isn't that good? Your broker doesn't have to call you every time a stock needs to be bought or sold. He is on top of your investments always, sitting before his computer screen, watching the markets all the time to make sure you are invested in the best stocks always. You can't do this. You are at your job concentrating on doing good work. Sometimes you are away on a trip or vacation and he couldn't reach you.

Isn't this type of an account efficient? Yes, it is the most efficient way for the broker to increase his commissions and for you to lose your money. It's a dream come true for the **broker** and a potential nightmare for you, the investor.

Let's now go back to the basic theme of this book:

More Transactions = More Money For the Broker

The retail side of the brokerage industry is founded on this principle. The broker gets paid when **you** buy and sell. He doesn't get paid when you buy and hold. Profits for his firm rise when the number and size of transactions also rise.

When you have signed a discretionary agreement, you have given your broker a serious conflict of interest. Will he buy and sell your stocks in **your** best interest or **his**?

Wait a minute, why are we going into this? It's your money and your interest always comes first. After all, if the broker doesn't perform well for you, you can fire him and go elsewhere. That's true. But what if the broker's daughter is getting married and he has to pay for the wedding? He needs to buy a new car. His wife is sick and has huge medical bills to pay. He wants to retire early and is focusing on making lots of money this year getting ready? He is just a little short of meeting his monthly goal for the bonus? He has a slow month and needs to increase his commissions to keep his job?

Here we are. Your broker has your authorization to buy and sell. You have 5 stocks in your portfolio. If he sold these and bought five others, he would have 10 transactions. If his average commission per transaction was $100, he would receive $1000. Your broker has ten clients with discretionary accounts. Assuming they have the same number of stocks, that would give your broker $10,000 extra for the month.

But wait! Your broker can't buy and sell just to generate commissions? That's not allowed by his supervisors who are supposed to monitor these things. How can the broker justify this action?

Very easy. Markets, companies and circumstances change. There are legitimate reasons for switching from one stock to another, so long as this decision is based on sound analysis. Judgment calls are involved with this process. Your broker's judgment, based on **his analysis**, is that it would be best for you to sell all of **your stocks** and switch your money into others.

Of course, he receives in this example an additional $10,000 commissions. But hey, he would have received this anyway. Right?

Based on **his judgment,** your broker **sells your stocks** and **switches** you into his stocks. This generates double commissions, one to sell and one to buy.

After all, it's just this month he has this extraordinary financial need. Guess what? Next month comes around and his financial needs are **still** there. So, he buys and sells your stocks again. He is hooked on the increased income. He changes his focus from investment to trading which can lead to turning over the stocks even more often than once per month.

Then, he realizes that the portfolio value has dropped 20% because the commissions charged to the account are now exceeding the trading gains. He now turns to trading vehicles that have the potential for very quick and large gains. One is **day trading** whereby he buys in the morning and sells in the afternoon. Another often used product is **options trading** which offer very high gains while even giving increased commissions per transactions. These have the potential of doubling in a few days or just a few hours. But options can also vanish to zero in the same short time.

While this is going on, you call the broker to find out what's happening. Your account statement is getting long and complex and it seems that the balance has been shrinking. After three months of this, you call your broker's boss to find out what's happening. By the time you meet with him, six months have gone by, your $100,000 is down to $25,000 and the broker is retired.

He made a lot of money on **churning** your account while you lost 75% of your assets. Now, you hire a lawyer and spend more money to try to recover your loss from the brokerage firm. Two years later, your lawyer recovers $50,000 from the $75,000 loss with $20,000 going to the lawyer.

How could this have happened? How could the SEC, the NASD or anyone have allowed this? While there are strict rules against **churning** and the brokerage firms discourage brokers from accepting discretionary accounts, there always are creative brokers who take advantage of the system. Finally, don't forget that the branch managers get overrides on the commissions generated by brokers.

The more commissions the broker generates, the more money the branch manager makes. Why should the branch manager turn away a good deal? He has financial needs also.

The basic problem is with the system of payment for transactions. The brokerage firms could eliminate this problem entirely by paying the broker based on his performance and the amount of money in the account, rather than only on transactions.

Never open a discretionary account with a broker.

"Opening a discretionary account with a broker is like the king giving his gardener the key to his treasure chest"
Gunther Karger

HOW CAN SHORT SELLING
BE DISASTROUS?

Short selling can often lead to big profits for the professional speculators, brokers and market makers. Let's get right to it and find out what a **short sale** is and how this dark corner of the brokerage industry works.

When you buy a stock, you buy it because you think it will go up. Why do you think it will go up? Because the company's prospects are expected to improve through higher revenues and earnings. You buy the stock because you are **bullish** on the company and therefore also **bullish** on the stock. When you bought a stock that's rising, you feel good and cheer it on. Why am I telling you something you already know? Because a **short** sale is the opposite to this.

When you sell short, you believe and hope that a stock will drop because the company's prospects are expected to get worse, not better. How does this work? It's really very simple. You call your broker and tell him you want to **sell short** 1000 shares of XYZ at $15. Wait a minute! How can you sell a stock you don't own? It's easy. The brokerage firm has lots of stocks in many accounts.

The broker will simply **lend** you the stock from another account and sell it at $15. You receive a credit for $15,000 in your account. This is a special credit and you can't spend it or take it out of the account.

Why? Because as in any loan, what you borrow you must return. In this case, you borrowed 1000 shares of XYZ through your broker from someone else's account. You must return these shares to the owner at some future time.

You **sold short** because you thought the stock was going down. You were hoping it would even crash. The further down it goes, the more money you make. You even cheer when it drops another point. This is reverse psychology at its finest.

Ok, the stock has now dropped to $10 and you think that the down move is about finished. You call your broker and tell him to **cover** your short sale. This means that the broker will go to the market and actually **buy** 1000 shares of XYZ at $10 and return the shares to the owner's account. You get the difference between the money you received when you **sold short** at $15 and **covered** at $10. This is a $5 per share profit less commissions in and out and gave you a whopping $5000 profit, based on the 1000 share transaction. Isn't that great?

Incidentally, the owner never even knew that he had lent out the shares. This is part of the agreement clients sign with the broker. If you have a margin account, the broker can use your shares for short sales. If you want to engage in short selling yourself, you must have a margin account. There is a very good reason for requiring clients to have a margin account to sell short.

Suppose you are wrong. The stock goes up, instead of down. Then, you lose as it rises. The higher it goes, the more you lose. Why? Because you have to buy it back at some point to return the shares to the owner. For example, if you sell **short** at $15 and buy back to **cover** at $20, you would lose $5000. You might even get a margin call as it rises because the broker has to make sure you have the money to buy the stock back. That's why the broker won't let you sell short without having a margin account.

There is dimension to short selling that makes it much more riskier than just buying the stock and owning it. When you buy the stock at $15, the most you can lose is $15 if it went to zero. But, if you sell **short** at $15 and go away on a vacation and find it went up to $35 while you were away, you lost $20,000 if you had 1000 shares in this transaction. If it went up to $100, you would have lost $85,000. In fact, the loss potential is theoretically infinite. When you **sell short**, you **cheer** when the stock drops and **cry** when the stock rises. Could you handle this difficult psychological situation?

Short selling is often used by professional traders, hedgers, market makers and even mutual funds. Individual investors rarely do this and when they venture into this reverse stock system, they often lose their shirts. They are at a great disadvantage because the short sellers often work together and control the stock prices through various manipulative procedures. The individual hasn't much chance here. It is very important to know about this so that you can detect when the **short raiders** invade your stock. The chapters on **manipulation** give very specific details on how these *Thieves of Wall Street* target your wallet.

"There is no fire like passion, there is no shark like hatred, there is no snare like folly, there is no torrent like greed" - Buddha

SHOULD YOUR BANK BE YOUR BROKER?

Leaving your neighborhood bank, just at the exit, the executive looking guy behind the desk smiles and greets you "How are you, Mr. Great"?

By the time he is finished, you have transferred $10,000 from your CD to *something* you don't quite fully understand. All you know is that it's the **bank's** program to increase your income above the paltry dividend the bank gives you on the CD that just matured. That's what you went to talk to the bank teller about.

What you got was a mutual fund, paid 8.5% commission and learned a month later that it was worth 20% less than you paid because the market went down and the commission. This was exactly what you didn't want.

How in the world did this happen? You didn't want to get involved with the stock market just now. Even if you did, you would have looked around a lot, especially at the no loads that don't charge commissions. You thought you bought another CD type of thing that just paid out a little more interest.

Then it hit you! How did that good looking guy know your name as you left the bank that day?

Here is **what** happened. You went to the bank to see about rolling over the CD that had just matured. The interest rates the bank paid were disgustingly low and you had asked the teller if the bank had anything better. She told you that someone would contact you from the bank to discuss this. She had picked up the phone and given your name to someone. Little did you know that the person she called was the guy at the front door **investment desk** to tell him you had a $10,000 CD that just matured. You just became transformed into a Dollar sign. No wonder that good looking guy was smiling and ready for you.

What really happened here is simple. In recent years, the banks have gotten into the securities business and sold stocks and mutual funds as discount brokers. Then, they got a bright idea.

Why **not** put investment desks near the front doors of the branch banks? That's where all the money comes in, with the bank's customers. This gave birth to the bank's neighborhood stock broker.

Then, the banks got another idea. Why not buy or start its own mutual fund? That would give the bank the fees customary in managing the mutual funds and additional income from the commissions paid for each transaction.

The customers would surely go for it because to the world, everything in the bank is **guaranteed** by the Federal Deposit Insurance Corporation, a branch of the US Government. Since the investment desk is **inside** the bank and the person behind it is a bank employee, customers would **instinctly** assume that anything done in the bank is **guaranteed** and **insured** by the bank. What an easy sale! Here was another great way for the bank to make extra money.

Suddenly, you now are the owner of a mutual fund you really didn't want. You especially didn't want the bank's own mutual fund. You wake up one day and hear the market dropped 100 points. A commentator talks about the continued drop in mutual fund values. You worry about what stocks are in the fund you have. You start to worry about economic indicators. You start to read more financial press and listen more carefully to the TV financial commentators. You subscribe to the Wall Street Journal and a few others. This is now costing you money and time tracking the markets. The reason you went to the bank was to **avoid** all of this. That's why you didn't call a stock broker, financial planner or any of those people. You were trying to avoid them because you weren't ready for them yet.

Yes, you just encountered the **conbank**, a modern name for **conman**. The **conman** is a simple crook who steals money from you and makes you feel stupid.

You were had and you know it. If you are brave and lost enough, you go to the police. If you are not **brave** and the loss isn't too big, you grin and bear it because you don't want to embarrass yourself for having been that stupid.

You don't want to admit to the world that you really could have been that stupid. The **conman** usually breaks the law and could go to jail if found and convicted.

What about the **conbank?** What's the real difference? You were set up. The bank made money on you. You ended up doing something you really didn't want to do. But, you did it anyway because it was done **in the bank** and what's done in a bank is **blessed**, **insured** and **guaranteed** by the United States Government. At least so you thought.

What's the difference between the conman and the conbank? Very simple. The **conman** is a thief breaking the law and belongs in jail. The **conbank** is a legal thief taking your money directly in the bank lobby straight from your own account. Moreover, the **conbank** relieves you of your money after charging you for checks, using the ATM, $20 for a returned check, $1 for a duplicate statement and more. It's even surprising that the **conbank** doesn't charge you admission for entering the lobby, using the toilet and parking your car.

Oops, I almost forgot. Now, some banks charge you $9.95 per month for accessing your account by using your own computer, right from your kitchen table. Yes, by using that computer to do your banking, you **save** the **bank** the personnel necessary to spend with you at the teller window or at the drive-in. The latest innovation was seen at a bank in Chicago which wants to charge customers $3 each time he needs to see a **human** teller. What's next? Could it be that the depositor will be required to pay the bank interest on deposits?

LESSON: *Enter your neighborhood bank with caution.*
Watch out for the investment desk!

THE NEWS RELEASE PROCESS

The public corporation is a business which generates and disseminates lots of information. Most of this information deals with operations and administrative matters, production schedules, procedures and all those things that make a company function. Generally, this is of little interest to outsiders and therefore rarely disseminated to the investment community. However, news such as financial results, projections, new contracts, labor disputes, senior management changes and mergers are of vital interest to investors. When significant events in these areas take place, it becomes essential to tell the outside shareholders and the investment community in general. Securities regulations require that this type of information is released nearly immediately upon the event, such as the signing of a major contract, a board decision to name a new president, etc. This can have a significant impact on decisions to buy and sell shares leading to rises and drops in stock prices. It concerns your wallet and therefore, you must always be current about what significant events are taking place in companies whose stock you own or are considering buying.

Let's look at the process of corporate information and how it works. Refer also to the **Survival Guide For The Investor** which tells how to get this information on a timely basis.

Public corporations are owned by the shareholders which may be anyone including the president of the company, board members, officers, mutual funds, yourself and pension funds. Shareholders are classified into two categories: **insiders and the public.**

Insiders include the president, board members, officers, key executives and outside persons who have specific knowledge of significant transactions that are about to take place. All others are the public.

Let's say you are a shareholder in public corporation XYZ. You call someone in the company and ask what the quarter's financial results look like or how a particular contract proposal for new business is coming along. This someone could be a friend who is a low level employee or the president.

If he tells you that the company is about to get a big contract for lucrative new business, you immediately buy more stock and then tell your friends. But, if he tells you that the company is about to lose a big current contract that will depress revenues for the coming year, you rush to your broker and **sell** your stock and **then** tell your friends. Chaos in the stock could result from this while you and a few others could profit handsomely by having had advance knowledge of this important corporate information. This is an example of using **inside information** and engaging in **insider trading.**

But fear not. Laws and procedures were established to assure that this could not happen. Unless of course, you happen to be creative, adventuresome and risk being a guest of the federal prison housing.

Federal securities laws regulate how information flows from the company to the public. These laws are supposed to protect the public from the abusive practices of **insider trading**.

An example of insider trading is when the editor of a major business publication **leaks** advance information to a few select brokers about a significant story about to be printed or an executive of the company telling a few friends about an imminent merger. Another example is an analyst at a brokerage firm which is about to issue a **buy** or **sell** recommendation on a stock telling this to his father who then acts by buying the stock **before** the public announcement.

These are examples of **no no's** on the **street.** Do these happen? You bet!. Are these illegal? Yes indeed. It's just impractical to monitor every situation in the whole country. There are far too many companies, brokers, individuals and opportunities.

Few men have virtue to withstand the highest bidder
George Washington

WHAT IS INSIDER TRADING?

The information flow from the **inside** to the **public** involves a few basic definitions. Since this often is a misunderstood area and is a critically important one, we will spend a little time on basic definitions. An investor just knowing these will gain a significant advantage in the elusive search for stock market profits. In the very least, the investor will reduce costly mistakes.

Inside Information
Information not yet disclosed that materially impacts the company, the value of its stock and the decision by the investor to buy, hold or sell the stock.

Insiders
Corporate officers and certain executive employees and their immediate family members who are in a position to know of or be party to important decisions. Outside consultants, brokers and officers of other corporations involved with specific transactions such as mergers, contracts and legal matters are also considered insiders as applied to those transactions.

Disclosure
The process of telling the public.

Public Information
Material information that has been disclosed to the public in an acceptable form. The transition from inside to public information has been made.

Insider Traders
Persons employed or affiliated with the company typically as officers, directors or key executive positions with the company buying and selling stock to the public. These persons must disclose their **intent** to buy and sell shares through filings with the SEC to make these transactions a matter of public record.

WHAT NEWS IS
FORMALLY RELEASED?

When a company has completed a significant event, federal securities laws require that the news is disclosed to the public very **promptly**. Examples of significant events, as defined by the securities laws are:

* Signed a contract for new business
* Appointment, promotion, death or resignation of a corporate officer or Board Member
* Definitive agreement for a merger, acquisition or sale of a major corporate asset
* Major new product introduced or discontinued
* Financial results
* Major lawsuits filed or settled
* Placement or retirement of major debt

It is evident from these examples that such news can have significant impact on stock prices. Therefore, the company is required, by securities laws, to follow certain procedures intended to offer **everyone** outside the company (the public) the **opportunity** to receive the news **at the same time**. This is critical because everyone has the legal right to receive the information **and** the company has a legal obligation to make it possible for everyone to receive this news **at the same time** to avoid giving unfair advantage to a few select persons.

HOW IS THE NEWS RELEASED?

There are two basic means of giving corporate news to the public. The first follows very specific procedures. The second is the informal **rumor mill**. You should always remember that information not yet officially disclosed through the legal process is **rumor**.

Equally important to **never** forget is that the official, legal disclosure is often merely the **confirmation** of the rumor. This brings us to one of the most important laws of Wall Street:

Buy on the rumor and sell on the announcement.

This applies to good news. If the rumor is about bad news, **sell** on the rumor and wait to see what happens when the news comes out. The rumor could be false or the news not as bad as the rumor implied. This leads to a chance to buy the same stock for less before it recovers.

Have you noticed that a stock moves on increasing volume **before** the announcement and then goes in the opposite direction when the news actually is announced? This means that somebody thinks that something is happening and that his information is so solid that he is putting his money on the table.

He is either buying or selling based on whatever he believes is his best information. Since what he has **heard** is not yet publicly disclosed, it has to be a rumor, events taking place in the industry or events directly concerning some other company that could have an indirect positive or negative effect on the subject stock. That's why you notice the volume rising ahead of the actual news. How can you detect this rising volume? This is covered in the *Survival Guide For The Investor*.

First, lets look at the **legal** and **official** means of disseminating the news. It's important for you to know what these are and how to work with them. I will again say what you will find often in this book:

Knowing how the system works is critical before you enter the system.

The following are the principal means of disseminating corporate information:

THE NEWS RELEASE is a short statement that is issued to the **wire services** for dissemination to editors of news bureaus like **Dow Jones** and **Reuters**, newspapers worldwide, analysts at brokerage houses, and magazine editors. The wire services, such as **PR Newswire** or **Businesswire** serve as gateways to the world. Once the wire service has received confirmation that the release has been received by its worldwide network, it immediately notifies the company the date, hour and minute this was done. This is the moment the information became transformed from **inside** information to **public** information.

DIRECT MAILINGS to shareholders is simply the mailing of the information to the shareholders and interested parties in the financial community. The transition between **inside** and **public** information is made when the letters are placed into the mailbox. The form of this communication may be a Letter to the Shareholders, a quarterly report in a fancy brochure or the Annual Report.

REGULATORY FILING WITH THE SEC is a report prepared in a prescribed format wherein public companies disclose information required by rule and law. The 10-Q is the report each company must submit to disclose its financial results for the prior fiscal quarter. The 10-K is the report for the prior fiscal year. There are other reports such as Form 4 used to report insider stock transactions and Form 8 for significant events like the appointment of a new CEO, etc. Schedule 13 is used to report stock holdings of 5% or greater and usually is filed by persons and other companies. This is very important in disclosures related to acquisitions and mergers.

The **news release** is one of the most important means through which the Company **discloses** to the public material information. Information that can have profound impact on the stock price.

The moment the Company has **issued** the **news release**, the information contained in that release becomes transformed from **inside** information to **public** information. It is critically important that you become aware of it and what information is issued as soon as possible.

Professional investors, traders, institutions and the news media receive it nearly instantly. This gives them a distinct advantage to act on the news right away. If possible, you should anticipate these releases in advance and learn the expected release date. Some companies actually tell the investment community in advance and informally, the date on which financial results will be released. If you have established communications with the company, you may also have the opportunity to get this schedule.

The **news release** can have instant impact on the stock price as it "crosses the wires" as today's efficient electronic communications make it available to those with the means of receiving it instantly. The trick is to be **plugged** into this system of electronic news dissemination.

The company prepares the text of the **news release** as close to release time as possible and in some cases, asks the corporate attorney to review the content. This is supposed to minimize the opportunity of **leaking** out the information and reduce legal exposure for the company.

WHY YOU MUST
GET THE NEWS QUICKLY

We now come to the important part of the process. This is knowing that the **NEWS** comes out as soon as it happens. Let's recall the **Law of the Street**:

Profit - commission = Loss + Commission
Here is Karger's corollary to this basic law:
Profit comes to he who gets the information first. Loss comes to he who gets the news last

It follows from the Law of the Street and its Corollary, that it is critically important to get the news as soon as possible after its release. Your financial health depends on it.

If you get the news when you call your broker to find out why the stock is down or up, it's generally too late. Someone else found out before you did and took advantage of it. Someone else won and you lost.

The trick is to be plugged into the *news system*. This is often very difficult. When the **news release** is issued to the wire services, brokers, investment professionals and editors receive it nearly instantly, within minutes. The resulting impact of the news can also be nearly immediate.

In one instance that I personally monitored, a stock dropped from $8 1/4 to $5 within 15 minutes after bad news came out on the wires. The company announced that it was taking a large writeoff in the next quarter. This news resulted in a 40% drop in value to the shareholder.

Equally important is to know when the news comes out in the form of a disclosure filing to the SEC. How would you know that the company made the filing? What was disclosed in the filing? How can you find out what it was?

When the Company mails out the quarterly report or a Letter to the Shareholders, how many people received this same letter via FAX the **same** day it was placed into the U.S. Mail?

The common thread about all this is that **everyone** has the **opportunity** to get the **news** at the same time. The question is though, how practical that is. Are you plugged into the wire services? Do you have a realtime stock and corporate news information system available to you? Do you have access to computerized information retrieval systems? The company is responsible for releasing the news. It's up to you to be smart enough to know how to get it as quickly as possible. Even if you are away on travel.

If you have all the above, you are among a very small minority of investors. But if you are, you are among that very small group of investors who have a much better chance of doing well with your investments. You are on the right side of the **Law of the Street**, the **profit** side.

What can you do to get as close as possible to the **profit** side? Refer to the *Survival Guide For The Investor* included in this book. This guide gives you specific procedures on how you can get investment information as quickly and reliably as possible.

The essence of knowledge is having it, applying it, not having it, to confess your ignorance

Confucius

YES, THE MARKET IS MANIPULATED

"My God honey, look at the paper this morning. The **market crashed**. It went down 150 points yesterday. How could this have happened? Just yesterday I heard on the news that the economy is doing better and business is picking up a little. How can the market go down so much in just one day, especially when we seem to finally be seeing some sunshine in the overall economy?"

"Wait a minute Sweetie, didn't some big Wall Street guru say just last week that the **market correction** is over and that we are headed for higher levels? Just now, I am reading in the Wall Street Journal that so many important economists and analysts think we are headed much lower. Do **they** know what they are doing? Should we sell everything we have or maybe buy more stock by increasing our loan on the house equity line?"

"Honey look at that company! Their sales last year doubled and the stock dropped from $18 to $13. A whopping $5 crash. How can it be that a stock drops at all when the company did so well"? "Sweetie, here it is! This is crazy though. The analysts expected the company to do just a little more than doubling in sales for that company. This means that the results were a little **lower** than expected." "But Honey, why would a stock drop when the size of the company doubles and the profits soar?"

"Wait a minute Sweetie. Didn't Greenberg or maybe it's Greenspan, the guy who runs all our money and sets interest rates get into the news recently? Didn't he just this week tell the Congress that the economy was so strong that he worries about runaway inflation?"

"I wish I knew who he talks to and what information he analyzes. All I hear about is more companies closing offices and laying off thousands of people. "

"You are right Honey, and what about the 8 million management people who had to settle for $5 per hour hamburger joint and sales clerk jobs after seeing their career crumble from $50,000 jobs?" Maybe Greenspan is confusing the Earth with some other planet in another galaxy. I just can't figure out this **stock market**".

What's going on here? How can stocks go down when the economy is supposed to be getting better? What's even more strange is that one day we are told the economy is doing great and the market crashes because of inflation fears.

Then, the very next day, we are told that the economy is slowing, we don't have to worry about inflation after all and the market roars up. How can the economy of the world's superpower change so drastically from one day to the next?

"I feel like I am being jerked around, being whipped into and out of the markets. Has the **market** gone manic depressant or do I need to see a head shrink to make me understand this crazy system so I can make some money instead of losing my shirt?"

"Or, are there a few **super thieves** at work here with a grand scheme to suck money from my pocket into theirs?"

Let's take a trip **inside the market** to see what **really** is happening. So we can go on with our lives and maybe still make some money in the stock market. After all, some folk do make money, don't they?

WHAT IS THE MARKET?

The **DOW** dropped 75 points yesterday and this is on the front page and on prime time TV news. What does this mean? What is the DOW? Who decides if the DOW rises or falls and by how much?

What is the DOW? It is nothing more than an index representing only 30 industrial stocks. This is minuscule compared to the 50,000 stocks that are on the market out there, somewhere. This index is a number called the **Dow Jones Industrial Average** (DJI) which is what everyone refers to when speaking about the **market**.

How's the market? The question should be: What is the **Dow Jones Industrial Average**? Did it go up or down? We have another index called the Transportation Index made up of 20 transportation companies, the Utility Index representing 15 utilities, the Standard & Poors 100 Index(OEX) and a host of others. But we will herein always focus on the DOW when we refer to the **market** even though it really represents a very small part of the **total market**. It is the very nature of this **DJI**, being very small in number, only 30 companies, that makes it easier for the manipulators to make the market behave in the way it does. The way **they**, the manipulators, want it to behave. This makes it easier for **them** to steal from you, the individual investor. The **market** is their **tool**, just like the safe cracker uses explosives to open the safe.

We should always be aware, that the DOW sets the **tone** of the overall market, the 50,000 stocks out there. Regardless if they trade on the New York Stock Exchange(NYSE), the NASDAQ, **Pink Sheets** or the regional exchanges (Pacific, Midwest, Boston, etc.). The DOW sets the direction and mood of the entire financial community. If the DOW goes up, the TV commentators, financial editors, brokers and analysts feel good. If the DOW goes down, they feel sad and worried. If the DOW goes down a lot, say 50 points in one day, they feel horrible and you see grave lines in their faces.

WHY

IS THE MARKET MANIPULATED?

Now, lets get back to the *thieves* of the **market**. How do they worm into the DOW and how do they reach into your pocket? Who are **they?**

This leads us back to the **brokerage industry.** Billion Dollar corporations and some lots smaller. A high rise downtown New York building filled with 5,000 high priced analysts, managing directors, chief investment strategists, directors of research and a host of others. It could also be a brokerage firm as small as a rented loft with one room staffed by just one person.

This leads us to the famous **Parkinson's Law** which was given to us in 1957 by C. Northcote Parkinson, a professor who taught business concepts at Cambridge University in England. This law is expressed as:

"Work expands so as to fill the time available for its completion."

Now, lets add **Karger's First corollary** to this important law as it applies to Wall Street:
"When the DOW tires into one direction and stagnates, forces are applied to move the DOW into the opposite direction, thus creating work for those otherwise sitting idle."

This leads us to **Karger's Second Corollary:**
"Work = Transactions = Money"

Understanding Parkinson's Law and Karger's Corollaries is very important. When you understand the principles of these laws as applied to Wall Street, you will have **mastered a secret of Wall Street that can save you a fortune and headaches you can't imagine.**

This knowledge can make the difference whether you retire in poverty or comfort, stay married or get divorced, keep your health or lose it. Not recognizing the existence of this concept could even cost you your life.

Lets go back to the chapter where we introduced the **Thieves On Wall Street.** These are people and companies who depend on one thing for making money:

Transactions = Money = Profits

When the DOW has been moving within a channel, that is, within a trading range, some investors get bored. Others get nervous. Most stop buying and selling stocks. The market has gone to sleep.

What does this mean? It means that the phone slows at the brokers' office. Business drops and profits slump. It also means that the brokers get nervous because the number of transactions drops and this leads to less income from commissions. The brokers fall below their monthly quotas and their jobs may be at stake.

They spring into action. Cold calling old lists and promoting exotic investment schemes. They look under every nook and cranny for investment ideas they can offer to the public. **That's you!** So they can reach their quotas set by their companies and keep their jobs.

But wait! They have lots of help. The brokerage firms note that commission revenue is slipping and profits are down. It's time to gas up and shift gears.

The firms' president calls an urgent meeting of its managing directors, vice Presidents of research and sales managers and gives them their marching orders:

Give our 50,000 brokers around the world something to **sell!** Teach them how to sell better! Get them moving! If you can't get them off their asses, yours will be on the street.

How is this for motivation? Make it happen or lose your job. And so, these very senior generals of the brokerage industry march out to set their legions of brokers on fire.

How can an army of nearly 500,000 brokers be set on fire? Simpler than you can imagine in your wildest dream. The brokerage firms instruct their branch managers to call a meeting of all brokers and read the **Order of the day:**

Meet your quota or clear out your desk!

How does this relate to Parkinson's Law and Karger's corollaries? The army of brokers are available and they simply create something to do with their idle time.

Work will expand to fill the time available.
Parkinson's Law

But wait! Doesn't this encourage questionable invest-ments conjured up by bored brokers and research analysts under pressure to produce? Right on!

Suddenly, the industry with all its might and an army of nearly 500,000 active brokers and thousands of product developers spring into action. Action designed to stimulate transaction activity in the **market**. Action to meet quotas. Action to keep their jobs. Action to make lots of money. Boy, do they get creative.

The DOW is a sitting duck. With the **right tools**, it can be **caused** to rise and fall. Importantly, when the DOW moves, other markets move also. The NASDAQ, bonds, futures, derivatives and many others. When the DOW moves up sharply, **greed** sets in. People watch it moving up and want to jump on the train to make a quick buck. When the DOW moves down sharply, **fear** sets in and people worry about losing what they have and sell. They think that the **market** is going straight down with no bottom in sight.

Either way, up or down, sharp movements in the DOW stimulates **transaction** activity. Individual stocks, bonds, options and all sorts of things get bought and sold. This leads to more **commissions** and more **profits** for the brokers and the whole brokerage industry.

Everybody is busy again, the order rooms are humming, money is flowing in. Sales quotas are again met. They get to keep their jobs.

What about the economists, analysts and research directors of Wall Street? Not to worry. When the market starts to have big swings, up or down, the demand for their services suddenly rises.

These Wall Street notables are sought after for their wisdom, write more research reports, get quoted in the Wall Street Journal, are invited more to TV shows and seminars. Occasionally, one or two even reach **guru** status and that's wonderful because it leads to talk shows, **money** and even **fame**. This can even lead to stardom and riches by being invited to advertise cars and shampoos.

The covetous man pines in plenty, like Tantalous up to the chin in water, and yet thirsty
Thomas Adams

HOW IS THE MARKET
MANIPULATED?

Let's get back to the time when the **markets** are quiet.
Like the still waters on a peaceful lake. Anyone watching
the lake will see the smallest ripple, the jumping of a fish
or for sure, the appearance of a two-headed monster.

The public must be encouraged to start calling the
broker with orders. Interest in the market must be stimulated. Mutual fund portfolio managers need to be awak-
ened. This thing has got to get back to the front pages
again to really get the public involved.

One day, a noted analyst at a major brokerage firm
appears on a TV panel watched by millions and says:

"The **market** has topped out, its cyclical trend points
to a minor correction and it would be prudent to raise
some cash." This gives a clue to the big institutional traders. They slow their buying and accelerate their selling
just a little.

The **market** drops 20 points. Not a big deal. A ripple
on the smooth lake. But still noticed by a few watchers.

The following day, Friday, the day after the **market**
dropped just 20 points, the Wall Street Journal has a big
article discussing the 20 point drop since it was just a little
more change than recently had been seen.

Several noted analysts and economists were quoted to
say that the **market** is tired and needs a breather. Some
say that the **Bull Market** needs a correction to set the
stage for future advances. Others explain the drop to
slightly rising interest rates.

The stock analyst following astrology and gazing the
heavens is quoted that Jupiter is in conjunction with Alpha
Centauri and this bodes ill for financial markets.

A noted international analyst blamed the Indonesian market which dropped big because old **KRAKATOA** erupted causing a local disaster on a small South Pacific island. An atmospheric researcher is quoted saying that this could litter the atmosphere with a huge dust cloud.

An expert in commodities reflected that this could have a significant effect on the **El Nino** which is an important world upper atmospheric phenomenon. This could impact the production of wheat, corn and other agricultural commodities. And yes, you guessed it! This could also lead to the possibility of a little inflation later in the year.

By this time, the tranquil lake was no longer calm. **Storm clouds** appear on the horizon and the waters swirl. Everybody around the lake is watching.

The third day after the initial comment by the analyst is Monday. During that weekend, major financial papers like the New York Times and Barron's further analyzed the week just past. And several noted commentators on prime time Sunday host programs focused on the weakening of the **market** giving their own views. By Sunday evening, lots of people were concerned about the whole economy, the **Market** and much more.

During that weekend, a few technicians on Wall Street worked overtime running their computer programs to see what all this meant. This created a sell program on the opening of the market Monday morning.

Just before the opening of the **market** on Monday morning, the Market Commentator on CNBC announces that technical factors are bearish and that he anticipates the **market** to open sharply lower. This is seen and heard by millions of people. The nervousness begins.

Exactly at 9:30 AM, also on CNBC, the floor of the New York Stock Exchange is shown with lots of noise and activity. You see a person on the balcony pressing a button. The **bell** rings loudly. Activity picks up with sharply rising voices coming from the floor of the NYSE. The **market** has opened. The system **springs** into action. The **thieves** have started looking for their daily prey.

On this cue, the **DOW** dropped 20 points within five minutes. Phones start to ring at the brokers offices. Clients were asking: *What's happening?*.

What was happening was that the **market** had dropped nearly 45 points during the first hour and still falling. The clients started to place sell orders and the brokers again got busy.

About 11:30 AM that Monday, the news was all over the TV networks and radio stations. The Stock Exchange had placed **Program Trading Limits** into effect because the DOW had fallen more than 50 points. Work stopped in offices all around the country. More people called their brokers. More sell orders were placed. **Panic** started. Brokers had to get their assistants on the phone handling their orders. The DOW dropped 150 points that day.

Presidents of brokerage companies gathered in board rooms and **cheered**. The brokers and their firms had a banner day! Transaction volume **soared** and commissions **boomed**. Market Makers stood on their heads cheering on the dropping bids on the NASDAQ and getting ready for the **margin calls** the next day. The **Market** had lost one trillion Dollars of **your money.**

Margin calls represent a wonderful opportunity for professional investors to pick up good stocks at bargain prices, as investors are forced to throw away excellent stocks at bargain basement prices. Margin Calls are also wonderful for the brokers. They generate bonus transactions because the client receiving a margin call must fork up more cash or sell his stocks. As discussed in detail in the chapter on the **brokerage industry**, margin calls can spell disaster and huge losses for the investor.

More transactions and more money from the client's pocket. Great for the broker and his firm. Now, let's recall Karger's Corollary:

Work = Transactions = Money

Yes indeed, interest had returned to the **market**. Transactions were up. Profits soar at the brokerage companies. The analysts and managing directors come into the news expressing their opinions. The editors and panelists on TV shows were again busy explaining the market's behavior thus justifying their jobs. They love it when the volume is high and the demand for their explanations is high. This gives them high visibility which is good for their careers and egos.

The President of the United States issues a statement telling us that our country is strong and then smiles as more people look to him with worried faces. Yes, he muses to himself,

"As bad as this thing may be to some poor folk (who just got poorer today), more people are now remembering that I exist. That's good for the upcoming elections."

What about the public? The public shareholders **lost** one trillion Dollars in value that day selling stocks in a panic.

Yes, there had been a raid by the *Thieves On Wall Street*. Your wallets and bank accounts became lighter.

You just witnessed how **Karger's Corollary** to Parkinson's Law works. Too many investment professionals were bored and available to do things and needed to make more money. Management of the brokerage firms and professional traders needed to stimulate action to make all this happen to keep their jobs. The capacity of the Securities Industry's **investment machine** had been idled and needed to be better utilized. **They** had leaped into action, using the means available to them.

Who are **They?** Let's move to the next chapter where we will meet **them.**

WHO MANIPULATES
THE MARKET?

We occasionally see reference made to a mysterious very small group of wealthy people controlling world economies. Books of fiction use this concept as a backdrop to plots involving high finance and world intrigue. Some non-fiction writings occasionally raise the question if indeed such **covert** group actually does exist. I mention this only in passing as food for thought. While the existence of such a distinguished group has never been proved, no one has proved its non-existence.

Let's not digress though. We are concerned in this book with thieves, the ones we meet. We are not blessed with the opportunity to meet the mysterious billionaires who occasionally gather with the **Gnome of Zurich** in the high Alps.

Who has the power to influence the markets? Are there really individuals who wield such enormous power?

Yes. At the top of the list is the Chairman of the Federal Reserve Board who is Alan Greenspan as of the time this book is written. Early in 1994, Chairman Greenspan shocked the financial community by raising interest rates a notch, only one quarter of one percent. Why? Because he said he wanted to stop inflation. This was strange because no one had noticed inflation amidst the continuing corporate restructuring, plant closings and massive layoffs.

The market dropped over 300 points during the following few months while he kept raising interest rates to fight this inflation everyone was now looking for but still could not find. Yet, no one could yet detect inflation as more companies consolidated and the army of restructured workers grew.

Then, mid year, after huge losses were seen in stocks, bonds, derivatives and all sorts of things, the FED Chairman addresses Congress to explain his actions because no one in even in the Congress could find the inflation he was fighting. He explained that **he** believed the **market** had risen too high and it was time for it to drop. But he also suggested that the **market** had dropped enough and that he believed the interest rates should stabilize because inflation had been stopped before it even started. He had launched a *pre-emtive strike* against inflation, to use his own words.

Yes, he indeed did launch a strike against inflation and it cost millions of investors dearly. He also managed to slow an economy which was just starting to see decent recovery, thus dashing the hopes of millions of laid off people who thought they might get jobs again within their lifetime.

The action by just this one Federal Agency and mostly just one person cost America's investors billions. Many portfolios dropped as much as 40% as some hysterical people on **Wall Street** declared that we now are in a **Bear Market** and that the **market** is headed much lower.

Did this action take real money out of your pocket? Did Chairman Greenspan influence the market? You bet it did. Did professional traders make lots of money resulting from his actions? Yes, without a doubt. Did the brokerage industry benefit through more transactions? Of course, all the way to the bank. Could the Federal Reserve be one of the *Thieves on Wall Street?*

The **market** then started to recover and again, we hit a bump in the financial road. The **Dollar** started to decline against the Japanese Yen and this was declared as inflationary. The **market** reacted very badly to this and again dropped to new lows. Again, people rushed for the exit, dumped stocks and worried about the end of the world as we know it.

We now come to the Finance Ministers of the seven leading world countries, known as G-7 or the Group of Seven. It was announced that these financial gnomes would meet over one weekend somewhere in Europe to **address** the Dollar's slide. At the conclusion of this well publicized meeting, they held a press conference with a proclamation that:

"The Dollar had dropped enough and that it was time for it to rebound".

This body of money power then instructed their Central Banks to buy the Dollar on the open market to actually raise its value. Do you smell a **thief** here?

WHAT IS PROGRAM TRADING?

Finally, we come to the computer. The computer programs that automatically buy and sell stocks and other financial products based on mathematical models. These programs and systems are managed and operated by specialists who work in **Wall Street** lofts and are hired by the brokerage industry. There are many exotic programs.

One program, for example, is like a basket of stocks, each basket representing $25 million of the Dow Jones Industrial Averages (**DJI**) of 30 stocks. This computer program **decides** when these baskets will be bought and sold on the New York Stock Exchange. When these programs are activated, many baskets are bought and sold very quickly. Keep in mind that one basket contains $25 million worth of the 30 stocks in the DJI or represent some other index.

Here is how it works and effects the market. Before the **market** opens at 9:30 or at any time during the day, the computer program and its programmer decide to **sell** 100 "baskets" *At the Market.*

This means that $2.5 Billion worth of 30 stocks making up the DOW are dumped at whatever price someone is willing to pay, at that time. This is just like having the real estate broker suddenly offering 100 houses for sale at an auction where they will sell to the highest bidder within the next five minutes. The value of houses in general will drop instantly due to nervousness about the real estate market.

Do you then wonder why the **DJI** drops 15 points within the five minutes when the market opens? Then, after the **DOW** has dropped 25 points by early afternoon, the computer sees a trading opportunity and places **buy** orders for the 100 **baskets**. The actual sellers made a huge profit during that day and in the process of making that profit, they scared the living daylight out of some folk.

Just like a drunk driver kicking down the accelerator on a high performance car and careening down the street, scaring the ordinary folk away.

Is this another **Thief On Wall Street**? You bet it is! Program trading accounts for as much as 15% of an average daily volume on the NYSE. This means that as much as 40 million shares are traded in this way. Think about this. A single person sitting at a computer keyboard, just like you might have on your kitchen table, has the opportunity and capability to trigger a cataclysmic event in the **market**.

Program trading was in large measure blamed for the infamous 1987 market crash where the DOW fell more than 500 points in one day, causing misery and huge losses to most investors. Congress has had hearings, many sound financial notables criticize program trading and yet, we still have it among us stealing money from us every day.

Who does program trading? You guessed it! The brokerage firms, insurance companies, hedge funds and the very big traders managing billions of Dollars. **They** receive while you pay. You might call these titans of the investment world **computer assisted and legally blessed thieves.** In military jargon, they are like *Sidewinder heat seeking missiles* targeted for the wallet in your pants.

We almost forgot our elected officials in Washington. Once, the President told a labor convention in Miami Beach that the United States should impose restrictions on Japanese imports. Within 30 minutes, the market drops 50 points reflecting fear of a trade war. The Agricultural Secretary goes on a tour of the Midwestern farms and tells the farmers that they aren't producing enough wheat and that the price will rise. The farmers cheer while the **market** drops 25 points on the fear of inflation in agricultural commodities. The Labor Secretary steps up on his raised platform and tells us about the wonderful increase in employment his administration has produced.

The **market** crashes 100 points on the fear of inflation until some economist notes that 90% of the employment rise was in minimum wage or temporary jobs and won't cause inflation after all.

Did these Washington folk cause the **markets** to gyrate up and down? Did these sudden swings cause you headaches, margin calls and a drain out of your pockets? Have the Washington regulators done anything but debate this problem in the hallways of Congress? Should these people be inducted into the *Academy of Wall Street Thieves?*

"Dare to struggle and dare to win"
Mao Tse-Tung

SUPERDAYS
ON
WALL STREET

The **DOW** races up 58 points. The **press** that day has articles telling us that we don't have to worry about inflation. The economy is cooling off and the data doesn't signal upward price pressures because of competitive factors in the marketplace.

CNBC commentators tell us about the good market prospects ahead, that we don't have to fear inflation and that the market will race to new highs very soon. The financial news, like the Wall Street Journal and others like it, have columnists giving good tidings for us, the investors.

Telephones ring across the country. Brokers call to tell us that we must hurry to get on the ship before it leaves. They tell us to get more of the stocks right now or we'll miss the last boat. Tomorrow may be too late!

The next day, within the first few minutes of trading, the **DOW** drops 40 points. CNBC calls the **Wall Street** experts to explain why this is happening. The commentators uniformly tell us that we should worry about inflation.

How can the **market** shift so suddenly and the opinions by the experts change so radically from one day to the next? There is a reason and we'll get to it shortly.

First, let's find out why the market really went up sharply one day and sharply down the next morning.

Do you remember the **computer programs** mentioned elsewhere in this book? The basket of stocks made up of the DOW 30 stocks worth $25 million per basket? Using this and other exotic computer based program trading systems, the institutions and the very big traders had a field day these two days.

One day, they **bought** the baskets of stocks and **sold** the index futures on those same stocks. The next day, they **sold** the stock baskets and **bought** the futures on the same baskets. To these traders, the transactions were nearly riskless and they, along with their broker friends made a pile of money.

This was an especially good opportunity because the very next day was **options expiration day**, known as **Triple Witching Day**. This is the day when stock options, futures and options on the futures expire. The program traders, institutions and brokers love this day. This is the day created by the securities industry out of the *love of money*.

The press makes a big deal of this scaring the average folk out of their wits. One day, we simple folk are told to buy because the economy is slowing and the next day we are told to sell because the economy is doing well. Then we are asked to understand what is meant by **Triple Witching**. What's this? A stock market or a bunch of wild haired witches flying on their brooms around their haunted mountain in the dead of night conjuring up wild schemes to drain our pockets?

Books are written about this. Financial commentators are paid to talk about it and editors are honored and paid for commenting on these mysterious things. Stock letter publishers tell us that we must subscribe to their **letters** to get the inside track on this mysterious market behavior.

Yes, the brokers love these days because **transactions** are up. Don't forget, brokers get paid whether you buy or sell. In some cases, the same broker will get a buy order from the investor one day because the mood is bullish and a sell order the next day because the mood is bearish.

The broker makes a profit both times. The market maker(a brokerage firm) makes a profit on the **spread** both times.

Yes, you might have guessed it!. You, the investor, lost both times. You were visited by another thief called **Superthief Day**. The day when the securities industry participants swoop down to drain more money out of your pockets. This day is the expiration of stock options, index options and futures resulting in a trading frenzy with a supercharge from computer programs. It's **Triple Witching Day** which happens four times each year on the third Friday of March, June, September and December.

What happens in the other 8 months? Not to worry. The brokers didn't forget them. They gave birth to **Double Witching Day** which occurs on the third Friday of the other months. That's when only two out of the three, Stock Options and Index Options, expire.

Why do you suppose this day is scheduled toward the end of the month? Brokers and their brokerage firms live by their transactions. Most brokers, and there are about one half million of them, have monthly sales goals.

It's important for them to achieve these goals not only to make good money for themselves, but also for their bosses who get overrides and their firms whose profits depend on them. The downside of not making their sales quotas is to lose their jobs. How's that for motivation?

The securities industry, consisting of the brokerage firms and their industry associations(NASD) and the Exchanges(the NYSE and others) got together and dreamed up a date late in the month and an event that would generate lots of transactions around that time. These transactions lead to commissions and an opportunity to make up for any shortfall during the first part of the month. This event would have **nothing** to do with the fundamentals of companies and their stocks, the economy, wars, floods, earthquakes or any such things that actually should have an impact on the market and stocks.

Where does this **extra money** come from? The money flowing to the brokers and their firms on these **witching days**? Why **you** of course. You, the investor, are the one who is motivated to **buy** the extra shares when the market roars up and **sell** when you get scared as the **market** crashes down.

The brokerage industry uses all its wares and tools that day. Computer programs, derivatives, $25 million stock baskets, futures, indices, analysts commenting on these and the whole power of the press including TV, Wall Street Journal, Business Week and a host of others. Everybody is working overtime. The computers are scheduled for maximum capacity. The whole system is fired up to generate extra volume leading to more commissions.

Can it be proved that the **Witching Days** were conceived in this way? Probably not. But it also can't be proven that this **is not** the way it happened. The fact remains that markets are much more volatile on these 12 days of the year, they do occur near the end of each month and they do generate extra commissions for the brokerage industry using techniques that have nothing to do with company fundamentals.

These concepts, strategies and methods are presented frequently in this book, dramatically and often in great detail. The purpose is simple. I have taken this literary license to help you better understand the **system** and show you the way to face the *thieves of Wall Street* and still make money.

"Opportunity makes the thief"
English Proverb

MANIPULATION
OF
STOCKS

A note about the word *manipulation*. You could use the word *influencing price* which has a softer tone. Let's define the term so that there will be no confusion. According to Webster's Dictionary:

INFLUENCE: Control, dominance, power, command
MANIPULATE: Control, exploit, maneuver, command

The difference between the two words is small. Both words mean that **something is being controlled to the advantage of the controller**. The opposite to this is that the action by the controller or manipulator is always to the disadvantage of the person being controlled. The **manipulator** or **influencer** have one major characteristic in common. **Power**. The power to effect change. As applied to the market and stocks, this means the power to cause a rise or fall in price. In other words, the **manipulator** usually is in a position of power to achieve this.

Stocks can be manipulated, just like the **market**. What's important to remember is that it is much easier to manipulate the prices of individual stocks than the market. The smaller the company, the easier this becomes. While the market manipulators are few in numbers and easily recognized, the **stock manipulators** are great in number and hard to identify.

Hold on here! How can we talk about stock manipulators? Don't we have laws banning this sort of thing? Of course! There were a few famous stock manipulators who were caught and went to jail. Like Michael Millken, the Junk Bond King of Drexel, an old and respected Wall Street brokerage firm. In just one year, he raked in more than one billion Dollars in pay for his service to the company. Where did this money come from? Our pockets, of course.

This does not include what his executive underlings and the thousands of brokers around the world made buying and selling his securities. Yes, he went to jail. An executive style federal detention center in a good climate and with the facilities of a country club.

After a little more than one year and paying over $500 million in fines, he now lives in a style we all envy. He still is worth hundreds of millions, and gives lectures on business to students of finance. What happened to his firm? It went out of business after key executives paid themselves handsome end of job bonuses.

There were others. Ivan Boesky and Dennis Levine were caught and convicted in illegal trading schemes. Today, they are out, having served their sentences in comfort. I doubt any of them are hurting financially. Yes, there will be a few others caught over time to make the federal regulators look good.

But for each manipulator you have heard of, there are thousands more who aren't even looked at by the regulators and law enforcement agencies. Stock manipulation can be easy to do and very hard to catch and much harder to prove. These are the **thieves** we will try to **catch** in this book. This gives you the chance to spot them and learn how the system works. Gaining this understanding could help you avoid making grave mistakes. This knowledge might even help you make money in the world of investments in spite of them.

WHEN ARE STOCKS MOST VULNERABLE
TO
MANIPULATION?

Let's take a look at **why** and **how** stocks move up and down. It's important to understand how the system works so we know when to be extra careful and be on the lookout for new opportunities.

Stock price movements result from a change in the balance between supply and demand. If a stock rises in price, there are more **buyers** than **sellers** at that given price. The stock will continue to rise until there is an equal balance between buyers and sellers. Transaction volume will decrease after this equilibrium is reached.

Then, there will come a time at which the volume is much lower than the average daily volume. This is the point at which stocks often are subject to a further move, up or down.

For example, a stock traded in the $15-18 range for several weeks with an average daily volume of 35,000 shares. The volume then gradually slowed over about a two week period to about 15,000 shares daily. Meanwhile, the price drifted down toward $15. Based on technical analysis concepts, $15 in this example represents an important support level for the stock.

If this level were penetrated to the downside, even by an eight of a point(Dollar), the price could easily and very quickly drop to the next lower support level. In this case, the next lower support level was about $12 per share.

How quick could this happen? It could start within minutes of the triggering event. How much could a stock drop when it starts a downward move? I once saw a stock drop $3 Dollars in 15 minutes after the news release hit the wires and was displayed on brokers' screens in thousands of offices across the country. This is the most vulnerable point in a stock.

This is the time at which it **is** possible to effect control. Here, the average investor stands to loose lots of money and very suddenly.

This price move could be triggered by:

* A NEWS RELEASE from the company
* A corporate officer, President, CEO or Director leaking information to a few select persons
* An article in a publication
* An analyst's recommendation
* TV commentator
* A buy/sell program by a portfolio manager at a mutual fund or money management company
* An individual initiating a buy or sell program
* A trader at a securities firm elects to mark down or up NASDAQ securities.

These triggering events can be very important in determining if a stock should be held, bought or sold and when. The understanding of these events is crucial to avoid being drawn into one of the many **schemes** available to the legal *Thieves on Wall Street*.

Read on carefully as we now will examine each of the above in sufficient detail to gain this knowledge.

What do most of these have in common? You might have guessed it! **The power to influence stock price movements.** You should always, in each and every instance, assume that there is a selfish motive behind the actions listed in the above table. It is essential, to your financial survival, that you recognize the existence of these actions, how they are devised and what can happen to your stock.

HOW CAN MARKET MAKERS
MANIPULATE STOCKS?

Let's review what a **market maker** is. It is a NAS-DAQ broker-dealer with a person sitting at the trading desk. This person is called the **trader**. A market maker could be a one person NASDAQ broker dealer where the owner, broker and trader is the same person. It could also be a large brokerage firm that makes a market in hundreds of stocks and employs a dozen traders who do the actual trading for the firm. You might want to refer to the previous chapter on the brokerage industry and go to the section on market makers which explains how the system works. Here, we'll just focus on **what** actually can go on within the system and how that can grab your money.

Stock XYZ sits at a $15 **bid** which is the low end of a $15-18 trading range. The volume has dried up. The chart indicates that $15 is on the right side of a **Head & Shoulder** formation which is very **Bearish** if the stock falls even a fraction of a point below it. The market maker is looking for trading opportunities and discovers XYZ. The price is $15 1/2 **ask** with the **bid** at $15. He believes that if he offers stock at $15, a retail customer, someone like **you**, is watching for an opportunity to buy the stock a little below the **ask**.

The trader was right because there usually is someone out there looking for a bargain. The 2000 shares offered by the trader was bought by another firm for their client. But, the market maker for that client then drops the **bid** to $14 1/2 as he wants to maintain the spread.

Suddenly, the screens at 100 brokers start flashing and a few customers call to see what's happening. Stock XYZ just **broke** below the $15 support level and people are worried about it going to the next **lower** support level which is $12. The bid now falls to $14 and the **ask** to $14 1/2.

The trader now offers another 2000 shares which are bought by another investor who thinks he got a bargain, because just the day before, he would have had to pay $15 1/2. Several other market makers now notice that **stock is being offered** and this is a signal of weakness.

Somebody is **selling!** Something is **wrong.** The chart has **broken** down. Several market makers now offer stock as it appears to go lower and so it does. This goes on for several days until the stock **drops to $12.**

Oops! I forgot to mention that the market maker who first offered the 2000 shares really didn't have the shares to sell. He sold **short** which means that he sold shares he didn't own. That market maker sold these shares with the knowledge that it is highly probable that they would drop and he could **buy back** at a cheaper price, the difference being his profit. He did the same with the second 2000 shares so he **sold short** 4000 shares receiving an average of $14 3/4. When the stock fell to $12 several days later and that was the level at which the chart indicated some support, the market maker **covered** his short position. This means that he actually bought 4000 shares for the firm's account to zero out his short position. At that time, he owned **zero** shares because that's what he started with.

Let's look at the math to see who made a profit and who lost. The market maker who initiated the short position and triggered the downward move, **sold short** at $14 3/4 and **bought back to cover** at $12. He **received** $59,000 when he sold and **paid** $48,000 when he bought the shares back to cover. His profit was $11,000 and since he is a market maker, he pays no commission. Not bad for a three day trade with **zero** investment! Several other market makers also profited on the way down.

Who did these market makers buy the stock from when it fell to $12? The investors, who became nervous and sold. Sound familiar? Who did these market makers **sell short** to while the stock was sliding down? **To you and other investors**, of course.

How do the brokers fit into this? They make out well because each time an investor or trader(not market maker) buys and sells stock, the broker and his firm are paid a commission. Since the volume rose dramatically during this slide, the brokers benefited from increased commission income and the brokerage firms enjoyed higher revenues from the increased number of transactions. Everybody benefited except you, the **street person** sitting on the curb wondering what happened.

Wait a minute! What about the **company** whose stock was being traded? Company XYC? Nothing was happening at the company during this hysteria. No news, no rumors, no industry events. All that happened was that one broker dealer decided to raise some money for his account by using stock XYC as his vehicle for doing so. Is this **manipulation**? Is there a **thief** out there somewhere?

WHAT IS "SHAKING THE TREES?"

Now, let's see if the market maker has other ways to suck money out of your pocket.

The market maker is usually very familiar with the company in which he makes a market. The trader gets wind of something good about to happen and wants to pick up extra stock for his inventory. He can do this in two ways. The first is to raise his **bid** as others will sell to him. This would be good for you, the investor because the value of your stock rises.

The market maker can also **drop** his **bid** which creates a nervousness in the market. A lowering of the **bid** suggests that something bad may be happening to the company or possibly the trader has sensed that a supply of shares are about to come to the market. Either way, this sends out a negative signal to the investment community.

Negative signals can cause more stock to be offered for sale at **lower** prices as traders and some investors want to take a protective action against a potential price erosion.

Let's go back to the trader working for the market maker. He drops his bid and some shares come to market at lower prices. He buys some. Then he lowers his **bid** again and more shares come to market giving him opportunity to buy even more shares at a reduced price. This can go on for some time and the price in a stock can drop significantly. A stock can easily drop from $10 to $7 in this situation. Importantly, the market maker can also initiate these actions on behalf of an important client who could be a big trader or a institution. Here is a real eye opener. Suppose that the market making firm is planning to issue a research report with a **buy recommendation**? Wouldn't it be good for the firm to accumulate shares at a lower cost **in advance** of the release of this report? These situations get preferential treatment by the market maker because they give a high transaction volume which lead to higher profits.

This is called **shaking the trees**. The market maker is shaking the dollar tree to see what fruit falls down to be plucked. The **fruit** is **your stock** he is getting cheaper than he could be if he didn't shake the tree. In the above example, the market maker has picked up 20,000 shares of stock marked down from $10 where it was before he started to **shaking the trees** to $7. His average cost is about $8 per share.

Suddenly, the news comes from the company. A new product is being introduced that will add significant new revenues and profits. The market maker immediately raises his **bid** and other market makers follow his lead. Stock offered at the **ask** price dries up and the **ask** price rises. The market maker still keeps his extra inventory until he feels that the price rise has run its course which is about the time the public has started to buy the stock. The stock is now up to $12 and the volume has expanded significantly.

The market maker then starts to **offer** his extra inventory and sells his 20,000 shares for $12. This little maneuver gave the market maker an extra $80,000 profit, not to even count the additional commissions he received through the increased volume. The market maker(firm) gives a small percentage of this extra profit to the trader who spotted the opportunity and did his thing. The firm, his trader and his brokers made out well.

Where did his money come from? **You!** You now ask yourself how you could have been so stupid to sell a stock just before it rocketed up. If you had been plugged into the information loop more closely, you might have also had wind of what was happening at the company and bought more shares as it dropped. But you certainly wouldn't have sold shares. This is another example how you, the investor, is often at a disadvantage. The *Street* shook your money tree. Would you call this natural market action or **manipulation?**

WHAT IS A BEAR RAID?

Bull means it's going up and when the **bear** comes, watch out. It goes down. When a pack of bears come your way, run for the hills. Your wallet is subject to a raid.

Here is how the **Bear Raid** works. Let's go back to the first example in the beginning of this chapter when stock XYZ sits at $15, on the right shoulder of a head & shoulder chart formation and is vulnerable. The volume is low and a small sell program could trigger a sell signal if the stock falls below $15.

A trader, who can be an individual speculator, a hedge fund portfolio manager or a broker decides that this is an opportunity to profit on the **short** side. That is, if he sold **short** 1000 shares at $15 and covered at $12, he could make a quick $3 per share profit. But this person is greedy and wants to make more. The chart says that stock XYZ could go down to about $9 if the selling became widespread. That would increase his profit to $6 per share.

It's now time for the trader to activate his **bear raid network**. He may be working with a newsletter writer who maintains a hotline and one or two market making brokerage firms. If the newsletter writer announces on his hotline that XYZ will go down if it breaks below $15, his flock will start to watch XYZ for a **short sale** opportunity. Then, one of the trader's market making friends drops the **bid** to $14 3/4. Another friend in his network sells as few as 100 shares at that lower **bid** which triggers the breakdown in XYZ. These pre-arranged and well planned actions activates the **sell** signal heralded by the newsletter editor.

The traders watching XYZ see this and start selling **short**. The price drops $2 for the week and shows up on the ten worst stocks which is listed daily in the Wall Street Journal and publications around the world. The newsletter writer is quoted as saying that the stock is weak, has broken down and probably is headed lower.

You and other investors in XYZ see this and think something is wrong with the company. You call your broker and he knows of no change at the company but does suggest caution until more information comes out.

Another investor becomes nervous because he just bought some other stock on margin, using XYZ as collateral and sees his collateral drop. He is worried about a margin call and sells XYZ to raise cash. A fund portfolio manager sees XYZ weakening and sells the stock from his portfolio. Why? Because he doesn't want to have his clients know that he still has XYZ in the portfolio when his report goes out for the Quarter. This procedure hides mistakes made by mutual fund portfolio managers. Did you ever wonder why mutual fund portfolios rarely have losers in the list of holdings when you get the quarterly report? **Now you know.**

The stock is now down to $9. You are nervous and have sold off one half of your position. Others have sold their entire position in the stock thinking something is wrong with the company. The **bear raid** network has stopped selling and price seems to have stabilized. Then, suddenly, you notice that XYZ makes a spurt up to $9.5 on increased volume.

Did anything happen at the company? It could be good news of a new contract or better than expected earnings. It could also be a squashed rumor or maybe nothing at all.

What probably happened was that the original trader and his **bear raid** network covered their shorts by buying the shares they had sold at much higher prices, thus nailing down their profits. They made an average of $5 per share profit while you and other investors lost that amount. Money flowed out of your pocket into theirs. The newsletter editor received free publicity and sold more subscriptions. Did the company fundamentals change? Not one bit. This had nothing whatsoever to do with the company.   You just were visited by another *Thief on Wall Street*. We call him the *Bear Raider*. He is just as dangerous to your wallet as a real bear is to your well being.

WHAT IS FRONT RUNNING?

You are excited! Finally, you have a great lead on a stock that could make it big. You call your broker and tell him to buy 5,000 shares of stock ABC. The **ask** is $4 and you place a market order. This means that you will buy the shares at whatever the **ask** is when your broker places the order. "Great, I'll get the 5000 shares at $4 before the stock goes up". Right?

Wrong! The moment you finished the call to your broker, he is on his computer looking up your stock. The fundamentals look good, revenues and earnings are on the rise and a few contracts have come in during the past year. The broker thinks Dr. Rich (that's you) must be onto something. "I'll buy some shares for myself and my special clients before the price moves up."

The broker places an order for 2,000 shares for himself at $4, then calls five of his favorite clients and tells them about this great new investment. Each of them agrees to buy 1000 shares and the broker places those orders. These are executed at prices varying from $4.25 to $4.50. The broker then places your 5,000 share order at the market and gets an execution at $4.75.

The next day at breakfast you open the paper to the stock tables to see what your new discovery did yesterday. "Great honey, look at this! The stock closed at $4.75. We made almost $4,000 already. I told you we finally are making it in the market."

Two days later, you notice that the stock slipped down a little to $4.5. Still, you *think* that you are making a profit after just a few days. You keep smiling until you receive your confirmation in the mail. The statement says you bought 5,000 shares of ABC at $4.75 for a total of $23,750 plus $500 in commission. You now have a loss, instead of the gain you thought you had.

You call your broker immediately because it has to be a mistake. You placed the order when the stock was $4 and that's the price you got, not $4.75. The broker tells you that the $4.75 is right because that's the price the stock was when it actually was bought that day. Yes, there was some fluctuation in the stock that day. But you argue that it was $4 when you placed the order.

The broker agreed, but also told you that you didn't place a **Limit Order** specifying the price. There really isn't anything he can do for you. But not to worry, he says. The stock will go up as it seems to be a real good situation.

The stock rises to $6.5 in the next three weeks. Your anger subsides and you stop questioning the broker. After all, you did make some money rather quickly. You calm down while your broker treats himself to a weekend at the beach, using the extra money he made on these trades.

You just witnessed **Front Running** by the broker. He bought **ahead** of you at a lower price before placing **your** order and took care of his friends and favorite clients. He then sold his 2,000 shares at $6.5 and made a juicy $5,000 extra profit plus the $500 commission he received from you. He stole **your** information, acted on it for himself **before** placing your order. He also **stole** a portion of your profit. Finally, the broker made extra commission on the trades he made for his favorite clients, on **your** stock and using **your** information.

What you just saw happens all the time. Not only on the buy side, but also when you sell. When the broker gets wind of a problem at a company resulting from a sell order from a client, he may either sell his own shares, sell short or sell shares in his favorite customer accounts **before** placing your sell order.

Although this is against the rules, enforcement often is difficult and the **front runner goes undetected and unpunished.** Did we just meet another *Thief on Wall Street?*.

HOW CAN STOCKS BE MANIPULATED
THROUGH THE PRESS?

"Honey, come quick! Your stock is mentioned on the TV and it sure sounds great. Tomorrow it will go up for sure. Start planning the cruise.? Let's buy another 1000 shares in the morning, OK?"

But when tomorrow comes, the stock starts to drop. "Honey, I just called our broker to see how our stock is doing, expecting a big rise after the great positive comment last night on the TV. Guess what, it's down. How can that be? How can millions of people hear good things and the stock drops the next day?"

Somebody already knew that the positive comment or article would come out. An editor wrote the article and had interviewed company officials and analysts over the prior two weeks. If it was a TV program, the person to appear was scheduled several weeks in advance.

Could it be that a few people knew in **advance** of the coming article or TV appearance and bought stock based on this prior knowledge? Then, when the news came out and the stock is up, they sold for a quick profit?

You bet it could be! It happens all the time. Illegal or not, it's the sort of thing that's very difficult to track down and prove. Editors have to get their information from company officials. Reporters may come and even take pictures. Analysts receive calls from the editor or financial writer asking for opinions. These people **know** that an article is about to come out and can easily check the publication schedules. They want to feel important, so they **tell a few of their friends**. Before long, lots of people know about it. Some of them actually buy stock based on this advance knowledge. This creates a demand for the stock **ahead** of the publication and this drives the stock up. By the time you read the article or hear the TV program, these lucky people have already bought their stock.

Now, let's look at what happens after you have read the story or heard about the company on radio or TV. The story really sounded great. A chance to get into a good company and make some money. You call your broker and buy 1000 shares at $8. You really feel great.

A few days later, you notice that the stock is down to $7. You call the broker and ask what's happening. How can a stock go down after good news comes out?

Here is what happened. The people on the inside circle knowing or suspecting the article or program was coming started buying at $5. When the news actually came out and the new buying started, it rose to $8, the time you acted on it. Then, the stock rose to $8.5 and stalled. That was the signal to the **advance buyers** to sell for their quick profit. So they sold for a quick $3 per share profit. They probably were selling the very shares you bought to squeeze a little more out of this situation.

These people know that stocks often fall shortly after the news comes out. Armed with this knowledge, they **sell short** when the stock rise slows and stops. This **short** sale was activated at $8, about the time you bought. When the stock drops to $7, they buy the stock back they shorted and pocket an extra point profit.

Let's look at the math in this situation. The advance buyer bought 1000 shares at $5 and sold at $8 for a $3 profit. Then, he sold **short** at $8 and covered at $7 for an additional $1 profit. These two transactions gave him a $4,000 profit for each 1000 shares. If he had traded 5000 shares, he would have made a $20,000 profit. That was great for him.

What about you? You bought 1000 shares at $8 and now sit with the stock at $7 for a $1000 loss on paper. You have two choices. Sell for a $1000 loss or hold for the long term because you feel the company is good and will rise back later. Unfortunately, you lost while the **insider trader** made a quick $4,000 profit and went on to his next prey.

You just became the **bagholder**. Yes, you also were visited by another *Thief on Wall Street*.

CAN YOU TRUST
THE PRESIDENT OF THE COMPANY?

Let's first ask another question: *"Can you trust the President of the United States?"*

Do you remember the campaign promises? Like health care reform. "Read my lips, no tax increases?" How often does the person on the campaign trail ever tell you what you don't want to hear like bad news? Even if it's the truth? Sure, you'll eventually find out. But the speaker won't have to face the eggs & tomatoes from the crowd. He'll be back safe and sound in his big office while you yell at your wife and take Maalox to calm your stomach.

Let's get back to the company president and any other senior corporate officer talking to an outsider. Remember, you are the outsider and the corporate officer is the insider. The legal meaning of this is very clear. The insider usually knows what is happening in the company. You, the outsider, knows only what you are told or what you can guess.

The corporate officer will rarely give you bad news. But he is glad to share good tidings with you. Especially the great prospects that lie ahead. Big contracts, good earnings, expanding markets and all kinds of good stuff. He will rarely tell you about lower than expected earnings, writeoffs, loss of contracts, resignation of a key officer or even a law suit. You learn such things from a press release which tells the world about it in an instant. When this happens, watch out. Stocks can crash within minutes. You could lose your wallet and much more.

Here is one example. The company president and his people were on a **road show** that lasted several months. They were visiting brokers, analysts and money managers in key cities across the U.S. telling them about the company's great future that was just around the corner. Some of these people bought the stock based on this wonderful story.

Investors who already owned the stock held on to what they had and even bought more, assuming that the road show would generate new demand for the stock. And that could lead to higher prices. A very logical move and one that should have a reasonable chance to work out.

After all, if the company management takes the time and spends the money presenting itself to new investors all across the country, how could there possibly be bad news just ahead?

Then, on a Monday morning, a trading halt was placed on the stock, pending important news. People got excited. Just the prior week, the management was in a major Eastern city talking to brokers. This could be the big contract everyone was waiting for. Or maybe even, someone has issued an offer to buy the company at a much higher price than Friday's close.

The trading halt continued through the morning. Still no news. People started getting worried. Why? Because no one can buy or sell during a trading halt. There is no liquidity. Your asset is frozen for the duration.

Then, just 15 minutes before the close of trading for the day, at 3:45 PM, the news came out and the trading resumed. The company had just announced a huge write-off of the very contracts that just the prior week were presented as the foundation for future growth.

Worse yet, the company announced a forthcoming restructuring with a big layoff and the delay of a significant increase in production capacity due to lower than expected sales for the period ahead. Finally, the company announced the retirement of its President, CEO and Chairman, the person who founded the company more than 15 years ago.

By the close of the day, just 15 minutes later, the stock closed down sharply at $5. Three points and nearly 40% below its close the day before. This was a total surprise to everyone, even to the President who obviously was done in by a young group who planned and executed a corporate **junta**. Just like occasionally happens in Latin America, when a president is toppled by young generals and colonels during the night.

Two months later, the stock drifts down to $3, reflecting the bailout by nervous investors who no longer trust anything the company says.

What could you have done about this? You should have sold all your shares immediately. As terrible as this sounds, it would have been the right decision because by waiting, you would have lost much more.

If you sold it, you could have used the freed up money to buy a new stock with much better prospects. If you made this switch, you would have rid yourself of a continuing problem, taken advantage of a new opportunity and been given a tax loss benefit on next year's Income Tax.

When unexpected and sudden bad news comes out, the chances are that it's the first of a series of problems facing the company. You are just seeing the first shoe dropping. You can be 90% sure that a second shoe will drop soon. Astute investors bet on this second shoe dropping and will avoid the stock until they see tangible signs of a turnaround, that the problem has been finally resolved. This generally can take months and even years. It might never happen and the stock will remain in the graveyard of stocks.

The company may not recover from the bad situation and could go into bankruptcy forced by the creditors. This is the worst of all situations because 99% of the time this happens, the shares go to **zero**. The lesson learned here is that you really can't trust the company's president. His interest is often adverse to yours and will tell you what's good for the company. This is not necessarily what's best for you, the investor.

A man who is always ready to believe what is told him will never do well.
Petronius (First Century)

WHAT ARE DERIVATIVES?

Derivatives made headlines early in 1995 and qualify as a newcomer to the **Thieves on Wall Street**. I would be amiss for neglecting to include this newcomer because *he* has found a way to **fleece** your pockets through the secure walls of your local governments.

First, let's find out what a **derivative** is by consulting our dictionary.

Derivative:
Related to something else, secondary, derived from another product, by-product, proportional to

To put this in simple language, if you want to buy a stock, you buy something **in place** of the stock that is mathematically linked to that stock. An **option** is an example of a derivative. An option is a right to buy a stock by a specified future time at a predetermined price. You buy the option at $2 per contract instead of the stock at $50 per share. If the stock goes up $2 to $52, the option also can rise $2 and become worth $4. In this example, you doubled your money trading the option but made only 4 percent if you traded the stock. If you bought a thousand options, you would have invested $2000 and made $2000 profit. If you bought 1000 shares at $50 per share, you had to invest $50,000 to make only $2,000. This is a huge difference in leverage and profit potential. That's what derivatives are all about.

The above is an oversimplified example of derivatives. The derivatives that became famous in 1995 were very complex financial instruments based on multiple relationships understood only by highly skilled mathematicians and computer programmers.

The value of these derivatives products typically are in the millions of Dollars. One estimate placed the total value of derivatives in effect early in 1995 in the Trillions of dollars.

Even the most sophisticated investment manager has great difficulty in understanding what derivatives are, how they work and their extraordinary risk.

Let's look at the risks. They are staggering, as the new financial debacle of the 90's unfolds. Orange County, California, one of the richest and financially most sound of all counties in the USA went bankrupt when it lost nearly $1.5 Billion early in 1995. When testifying on his own behalf, the county's treasurer of nearly 20 years admitted that he did not understand the derivatives he bought on behalf of the County's investment fund. He even acknowledged that he did not recognize the enormous risks associated with derivatives. This is a person who had been respected throughout the country. The very one who successfully led the county on a positive financial track for many years.

Late February, Barings Bank, a renowned British investment bank lost its entire capital of about $1 Billion and closed its doors looking for a buyer. This is the very bank that financed Napoleon and the famous Louisiana Purchase from France by the United States. Barings had been in business for nearly 250 years and to this day served the financial needs of the British Royal Family. What triggered this world financial disaster? A 28 year old trader in Barings Singapore office invested heavily in **derivatives** betting that the NIKKEI index on the Tokyo Stock Exchange would rise. Instead, it fell. He bet the wrong side and lost. The loss was so big that it broke the bank. What was the outcome? A Dutch financial house bought Barings for One(1) British Pound, about $1.60 U.S. Dollars plus its obligations.

Across the United States, financial managers of cities, counties, banks and corporations, are reporting large losses from derivatives. A financial manager of a small Midwestern city acknowledged losing $6 million and that's a lot for a small town. A public corporation announced losing over $100 million wiping out the entire profit from one of its major divisions.

It is difficult to understand by even the most experienced people how these things could have happened. What is more important, how it could be **allowed** to happen.

Yet, the answer is simple. It goes to the very foundation of the securities industry as it today exists. The answer is given in many ways throughout this book. I introduced it in the **Preface**. The answer was also in the chapter called **Introducing the Thieves on Wall Street?**.

Yes, you guessed right. It's the brokerage industry again. Just plain stocks, bonds and futures were no longer enough. The urge to increase commissions and transactions led the most creative arm of the brokerage industry to engage space scientists, Ph.D. mathematicians and computer programmers to design a whole new array of products. We know them as **derivatives**. The ones we just discussed. Another advanced product of the research and development departments of the brokerage firms.

The largest and most respected brokerage firm, through its star institutional salesman introduced the treasurer of Orange County to derivatives. Legions of institutional brokers across the nation and the world called on investment managers at pension funds, mutual funds, school boards, corporations and city governments. Derivatives were presented as an answer to increase yields while the interest rates were low. Board rooms of the brokerage firms looked to derivatives as an answer to their prayer for a new product that generates higher profits through greater commissions.

The **sell** was easier as the brokers would offer this product to managers controlling large sums of money. The jobs of these investment managers depend on doing better each year. These people can make a decision more easily than an individual. It's **not their money**. They just manage a pool of money. **Your money!**

Yes, it's your money. Money you placed in the bank, in your mutual funds, in your pension fund and even, in your favorite company. Your money that someone else controls and invests.

When these managers announce losses resulting from derivatives, the value of your mutual fund or pension account drops and your stock sinks when lower earnings are announced. Yes, you too can lose from the derivatives and you didn't even know you had them. Most of you probably didn't even know these existed.

Who profited from this situation? Those who created these products and sold them. These are the architects of financial instruments and yes, we are talking about the brokerage industry. This includes especially the brokers who sold them and collected huge commissions.

Are we finished with this relatively new financial product? Not by a long shot. Derivatives in some form will be with us for a long time. The titans of Wall Street continue to bless them as good. The brokerage industry only has to do a better job of educating investment managers about the risks.

You just met a new Thief on Wall Street

A substitute investment is like flying a paper airplane instead of a real one

Gunther Karger

SURVIVAL GUIDE
FOR
THE INVESTOR

We have talked about the *Thieves on Wall Street*. The people calling from boiler rooms. Penny stock brokers making cold calls. Company presidents lying straight into our faces. Traders and market makers shaking the trees stealing our stocks at bargain prices. News editors in collusion with short selling networks. We have talked about the Federal Reserve Board Chairman jerking the markets wildly scaring the ordinary folk. Even the President of the United States joins the circus on rare occasions, trying to calm us down and often makes things even worse. If that's not enough, we face Triple Witching Day four times each year adding to our regular Halloween woes. Is everyone involved with investments a *thief* as defined in this book?

Absolutely not. In fact, many of the *types* we have identified don't even know they are part of any scheme to pluck money out of your pocket. Many of these people are working hard to make a living within the system as it exists. Some of them even become victims themselves on occasion.

Despite all this, can we still want to get our fair share in Wall Street? After all, it's our money these vultures play with. We want to have a chance at making money too. We want to make sure there is something left for us on the table. After all, the brokers get theirs, the investment bankers line their pockets, the company officers get their golden parachutes and the regulators get their fat pay checks and then sail into the sunset on their golden wings. Wings filled with gold from our tax Dollar.

Is there still a chance for us? The ordinary folk? The ones who have toiled a lifetime and placed our financial resources on Wall Street? How can we improve our odds? What can we do, as individuals?

Plenty. The first step is to **understand the system**. What it is and how it works. We have to know how to identify the faces of Wall Street's people. Who they really are, whose interest they represent and how they make money.

This, we already have done. I wrote this book to make this possible. I said it like it is, so **you** would know **how it is.** Brokers and others in the investment community probably won't like it. They might even offer to buy all the books printed so none will reach you. So their schemes can be used a little longer. But rest assured, the more they buy, the more our publisher will print.

Now, we will go through specific steps **how we can work within this system**. So that we too can make money. Some of you may decide, after reading this book, that Wall Street isn't for you. You may decide that it's better to place your money in the bank or even in a box underground to protect it from these thieves. That's OK. Better having money in a bank at 5% or a Treasury Note at 6% and making sure you don't place it at risk with these thieves. This way, you at least will not lose your money. You just won't make any. You might just barely keep up with inflation.

The **Investor's Survival Guide** is organized like a handbook giving specific guidance, step by step. This guide tells you:

HOW to react to the markets
HOW to get and handle the news
HOW to select brokers
HOW to work with the brokers
HOW to communicate with the company
HOW to select stocks and mutual funds
HOW to work with a margin account
HOW to deal with broker problems.
HOW to recover money lost with your broker

The **Survival Guide for The Investor** is an easy and handy reference that can help you through difficult times. Whenever in doubt, just look up the section on the subject and chances are that you will get some answers.

Remember though, that these are suggestions dealing with average situations. There will be exceptions as individual situations may be unique. When in doubt, just use your common sense and refer back to the section of this book dealing with the main subject. Call your broker and ask questions. Visit your library which often has a wealth of information. Call the company. You should also consider consulting with an attorney when you feel that you need legal help.

WHAT TO DO
WHEN THE MARKET SWINGS

Always remember that the tone of the market is set by the **Dow Jones Industrial Averages** commonly known as the **DJI**. While this index represents only 30 stocks out of more than 50,000, it is the market's **altimeter**. For those of us who aren't pilots, the altimeter is the instrument in front of the pilot's panel telling him how high the plane is flying. The DJI index has risen over the very long term. In the 1930's, the DOW was about 200 and during 1994, it reached 4,000. Yes, there were many ups and downs along the way and there will be more swings as we move forward in time.

As long as the world maintains a capitalistic system, there will be more companies trading on the many exchanges in more countries and this trend is expanding rapidly. Just one example is China, with its billion population. Companies are being privatised and its economic system is starting to look like those of the West. The former Soviet Union is in its infancy turning to the capitalistic system with Eastern Europe well along the way. Latin America is on the threshold of a major long term economic expansion, having now rid itself of dictators in all but one country. This leads to the expansion of investment opportunities. More companies, changing technologies and more informed people. These are positive factors supporting the expectation of a long term continued uptrend in world markets.

These opportunities will expand at an increasing rate as the world continues to shrink thanks to modern communications. News breaking about events anywhere in the world now is available to us regardless of where we are. Information transmitted via telephone, cellular telephone, cable, satellite or radio can today reach us whether we are in the office, at home, in the car, airplane or boat and yes, even on the beach.

We must always keep these perspectives in mind when we see wild swings in the market averages and hear the commentators tell us that Armageddon is near. If the President of the United States were assassinated, there will be a new president and the country continues. If a war breaks out somewhere in the world, the world will **survive** as there have been wars since the beginning of time all the way back to the cave man.

When the market experts tell us that a bear market is ahead, remember that most forecasters are usually wrong. But even if they are right, a bear market measured in context of the long term is only a temporary correction in a long term uptrend.

When the market **plunges** 100 points in one day and this headline faces you in the next morning's newspaper, keep in mind that it may have happened during the last 30 minutes the prior day. The drop could have been triggered by computer programs that have nothing whatsoever to do with business conditions or company prospects.

When there is a major disaster, like earthquake, hurricane or bankruptcy of a major corporation, you should remember that these are temporary situations. These have been with us for generations and will continue beyond our lifetime.

If you **worry** about the **end of the world**, a nuclear winter, the collapse of the free market system or maybe even an invasion by aliens, stop right there. There is nothing we could do about that, even if we dug bunkers and lived underground. Except, of course, for praying to the Lord of our choice.

Finally and this is very important. You should never forget that the **market is made up of stocks.** Some stocks rise in bear markets while others drop in bull markets.

When you invest in stocks, you invest in companies, unless you are adventuresome and dare speculate in derivatives, hedges and index options, all of which the prudent investor should avoid. These financial instruments are very sensitive to market swings, interest rate changes and world currency fluctuations as well as weather conditions.

If you venture into this world, you are about to get the roller coaster ride of your life and you'd better strap in and reserve a funeral date.

The investor should keep three very important rules in mind at all times. This will help you keep your sanity while helping you to **avoid costly mistakes.**

* **The market** reacts to the mood accepted by the financial community at any given time. This mood can change in one hour or last for months.
* **The Market** is made up of stocks and that's where you put your money.
* **Establish** a basic investment strategy and always refer to it before reacting to any situation, especially panic situations.

The following page gives you **five cardinal rules** for reacting to market swings. These are simple rules and easy to follow. You would be surprised though, how many people ignore these rules and lose their shirts. Don't you be one of them!

RULES FOR REACTING
TO
THE MARKET

ONE: Don't react to market panics unless these represent an opportunity based on your investment strategy. Be prepared to buy more stocks when the market crashes. This is bargain hunting on super sale days.

TWO: Don't over-extend yourself by being too heavily invested, especially on margin, which could force you to sell during market panics. You will lose while your broker gains.

THREE: If you are in mutual funds, which are very sensitive to market swings, you should be very informed about market trends and have a strategy of switching into and out of certain funds based on market timing. Why? Because mutual funds are a basket of securities that often fluctuate significantly with the markets. Use a family of no load funds that allows you to switch between funds at very low cost.

FOUR: If you have a diversified portfolio of more than 10 stocks, you should be more sensitive to market swings, since you in fact have a mini mutual fund. Sell a percentage of the portfolio after the market reaches new highs and interest rates start to trend higher. Buy a percentage of the portfolio's value after big market drops and interest rates start to trend lower or are stable.

FIVE: If you are into bonds, always remember that **bonds rise when interest rates fall and drop when interest rates rise.** These can be long term trends and you should be familiar with interest rates and monetary conditions. The broker may tell you not to worry because the dividend is fixed. That's true. But what good is a steady dividend when the value of your bond has dropped in half?

HOW TO SELECT
AND
WORK WITH BROKERS

Knowing how to select and work with brokers is one of the most important aspects of investing in the stock market. Sometimes even more important than knowing which stocks to buy. Knowing how to place orders and when to buy and sell is essential to have a chance at making money on Wall Street. This knowledge is critical to preserving your money and minimizing losses.

Look at it this way. It's like buying a factory. You have to know a lot about how the machines work and operate the business. Working with brokers is no different. You must know how they operate so that the outcome is to your benefit. The system is structured so that you **must** use brokers. You really have no choice.

We have already learned a lot about the brokerage business in this book. We made a big thing about how they make their money and how creative they can be in making very big bucks for themselves. We have said, in as many ways as possible, that these bucks come right out of your pockets. Their income is directly linked to the number and size of the transactions you do. A broker who is excellent in picking stocks and giving you this information will go broke and be fired if he doesn't get you to buy. You must always know this when you work with brokers. **No transaction, no food on his table.** Does this mean that all brokers are bad and just after your money? Not at all. There are many very good brokers.

You just have to remember that there is an inherent conflict of interest between you and your broker. The following questions should always be at the top of your head when you and your broker are discussing the buying or selling of a stock:

1. *Is the proposed transaction best for my investment strategy or best for the broker's need to meet his monthly sales quota?*
2. *Does the brokerage firm have a need to sell this stock as a result of a prior stock offering or relationship with a client company?*

Whenever you feel the need to make a decision based on your broker's recommendations, ask yourself the questions just presented. You can't ever ask these questions often enough. It should be automatic. Asking these questions should be your basic instinct.

Selecting a broker is an important step in your investment process. Choosing the right broker probably will make the difference between making or losing money. It's not only **who** you pick. It's the **type of broker** you choose. These are vital decisions and should be an integral part of your investment strategy.

Brokers provide the following two basic services and it's very important that you fully understand what these are and the difference between them:

Transactions - Buy and sell orders
Information - Recommendations, research

You must use a broker for transactions because the system is structured in this way. However, you are not required to use brokers for information or advice. These can be obtained **separately from independent sources,** such as doing your own research and subscribing to services specializing in investment research.

The ideal situation is to **separate** transactions and information. To put this in another way, get transactions from your broker but get information from an independent source totally separated from your broker.

Different types of brokers are available offering a variety of services at different prices. When you go shopping for a broker, it's like going to the financial supermarket. Today, you have a certain need and you go out and buy what's best for you today. Tomorrow, your needs may change and you again go shopping to the financial supermarket for something different. Your needs may change with time and as your knowledge improves.

FULL SERVICE BROKERS

If you are new to the investment arena and want to learn or if you don't want to spend the time doing your own research, you should select a broker in a well organized full service brokerage firm. You need all the information and help you can get and have someone you can talk with as often as you feel the need. The following are rules for selecting the full service broker:

ONE: The brokerage office should be reasonably nearby making it easy for you to visit during days.

TWO: Speak with the manager and tell him about your needs and goals. He will introduce you to a broker in the office. Do this with several offices and take your time before selecting a broker.

THREE: Be up front with the broker about your needs and your expectations.

FOUR: Tell the broker, right up front, that you don't expect discounts on his commissions, that you want to be sure he gets properly paid. Tell him also, that you expect a good and honest service. Most people will do the opposite. The first thing they do is ask the broker how much discount they can get. This gets both off to the wrong start and you will pay dearly as long as the relationship lasts. Don't make this big mistake. You can't expect to get good service at a discount.

FIVE: Learn a great deal about the broker. You will spend time with him and give him lots of information about yourself, as you develop a relationship.

SIX: Check with the NASD for any possible violations filed against the prospective broker and the Branch Manager. The number to call is 202-728-8039.

SEVEN: Check with your friends and acquaintances to learn if they had any experiences with the broker and his office.

EIGHT: Don't use a friend or relative as a broker. The time will come when you must decide to change brokers or the type of service, as you gain more experience. You don't want friendship or relations to get in the way of investment decisions, **ever.**

NINE: Once you select the broker, don't commit all your funds earmarked for investments to that account right away. Give yourself some time to test his recommendations and your ability to get along with the broker.

TEN: Spend a little time checking out the new broker's recommendations. If necessary, go to the library and look up the company in Standard & Poors or other investment reference. You could even call the company and ask for the Investor Relations Department or the Chief Financial Officer and get some questions answered. If you have any questions after verifying some of the information your broker gave, call your broker and ask. If he resents you checking up on his recommendations before buying the stock, look for another broker. It's **your money and your risk.** You have every right to ask questions and verifying basic information until you gain confidence in your broker. That's what you are paying him a full service commission for. You are completely entitled.

ELEVEN: Subscribe to one financial newspaper such as the Wall Street Journal or Investors Daily and occasionally get a weekly financial magazine such as Forbes or Business Week.

TWELVE: Read the business section of your local newspaper. You have placed your money in the market and you should keep up with that market place.

Full service brokers may discount commissions under certain circumstances. You may get a discount if you have a big account and trade frequently. You, the client, must bargain with the individual broker to get any discount and that puts you at a disadvantage. If you have a small account, say less than $25,000 and don't trade frequently, the broker won't give you a meaningful discount unless you really put the pressure on. You then run the risk of receiving poor service. Like slow call backs, poor executions and in general, the least service the broker can get away with.

You bargained with his monthly paycheck and he resents that. Now is getting back time. I previously suggested to **never** bargain with a full service broker. If you need his services, pay for them. **If you don't need the services, don't use a full service broker.**

As a general rule, use the full service broker to learn how the system works. If the broker does real well for you and you trust him, stay with him. But never, ever, try to get a discount on anything he offers. That's like asking for a discount from your lawyer, doctor or any other professionals. They resent bargaining but may reluctantly give you a small discount. However, they will **never** forget that you asked. They will never go the extra mile for you, even when you might need that help.

DISCOUNT BROKERS

If you have a reasonable knowledge of how to deal with the securities industry and know how to place orders, this may be for you. You can go there, see their faces, ask some questions about transactions, get your checks, deliver your securities, etc. But there is **no** advice. You are dealing with salaried people and their job is to give service, not a sales pitch.

These brokers may also let you trade no load mutual funds at a small transaction fee. This can be very advantageous because there may be occasions when you want to shift from mutual funds to stocks and vice versa. This is especially important when you allocate your assets based on market timing.

You should use the deep discount brokerage firm if you know how to place orders, how the markets work and how to get **your own research.** These firms provide **transaction services** by allowing you to place orders in several ways. First, you can simply call the firm on the telephone and tell the broker what you want to do. You may want to buy or sell, check your account status or get quotes on stocks. This person is a licensed broker who understands the procedures for placing orders. However, he is salaried and is under strict instructions to never give any investment advise. He is there only to facilitate your transactions. It's almost like ordering a product on a toll free 800 line.

Deep discount brokers typically charge very low transaction fees. Commissions of less than $50 are normal vs the $85 plus per trade for the discounters with walk in offices.

Many deep discount brokerage firms also have a system whereby you can place your order, check for quotes and get account balances by using the telephone keypad the broker's interactive voice mail. The brokerage firms are increasingly offering a service where you can use your computer to do everything. This is very efficient as you can even use a portable notebook computer with a modem no matter where you are.

All discount brokers will confirm your transactions on the telephone if you wish and send you written confirmation statements within a few days. If you use your computer, the confirmation is provided almost immediately while you remain online. You will also get the regular confirmation statement in the mail a few days later as well as comprehensive monthly statements. These services are just like the full service brokerages.

If you have questions about your trade or your account, the deep discount firm gives you another 800 number to call. This is called customer service which helps you with everything except taking orders for trades. This is the number you call to request for funds, transfers and anything to do with your account. Many deep discount brokers even offer checking services and debit cards which can be very convenient. Again, the full service firms also offer these services. You lose nothing in the service area.

What about commissions? **You can save a lot**. A transaction that can cost $150 - $1000 at a full service broker could cost as little as $25. For example, you might pay about $325 to buy or sell 1000 shares of a stock priced at $20. The same transaction could cost you as little as $25 at a deep discount broker. Remember also that what you buy you must sell. The $300 saving per transaction then becomes a $600 savings for the round trip trade. That's a lot of money. You could pay for several stock letters, independent research reports and financial publications for the savings of just one such trade. You would also get your investment information from a source totally independent from the broker which is exactly what you should want.

Let's take another example of a low priced transaction of 1000 shares at $5. The full service commission would be about $140 vs the $25 at the deep discounter. Notice that the deep discounter gives a flat transaction charge while the full service broker charges more depending on the value of the transaction. The truth is that the expense to the broker is a **per transaction** cost which is passed on to the customer at a reasonable markup.

One trade, one ticket, one confirmation statement, one call. It has little or nothing to do with the number of shares or dollar value.

Some deep discount brokers charge on a per share basis but with a very reasonable minimum commission rate. For example, one very good deep discounter charges 1.5 Cents per share for NASDAQ stocks and 2.0 Cents per share for stocks listed on the exchanges (NYSE, etc.). As in the flat rate schedule, there is no penalty for dollar value. For example, a 1000 share NASDAQ transaction would be 1000 X 1.5 Cents = $15. But since the minimum commission might be $35, that's what is charged to the customer. It doesn't matter if the stock is $1 or $100.

Another benefit in using a deep discounter is that you avoid some of the schemes made possible when you deal with a brokerage house that makes markets in stocks. Deep discounters generally don't get involved with these things nor do they do investment banking.

Deep discounters simply provide transaction and account related services and charge you a reasonable fee for these. Don't forget that you are only buying transactions from a deep discount broker. Advice and research you get elsewhere.

For example, if you placed an order for a NASDAQ stock with a spread of 50 Cents, the deep discount broker is supposed to go to the NASDAQ to get you the best price, which sometimes can be below the **ask** price. If you placed the order with a brokerage firm that also makes a market in the stock, you will rarely get a price below the **ask** and you will always be subject to games and manipulations made possible by the system.

If, for any reason you don't like the service at the deep discounter you selected, look for another and just transfer the account. This can be very simple and usually only involves filling out a short form, attaching a copy of your last statement and the **new** brokerage firm will handle the rest. This procedure is computerized within the industry and should take no more than 2-3 weeks and cost you nothing.

You don't have to explain your action to any broker and feel embarrassed about it. You just shop for the best service at lowest cost. The financial magazines, newspapers and TV programs are full of ads for these brokerage services and they are getting better all the time.

Just remember, when you use a deep discount broker, **you** are the **captain** of your ship. **You** decide where you are going. **You** get the benefit of your own work.

The most important benefit of all is that you will be much better informed and thus able to make better investment decisions.

One of the more difficult investment decisions you often are faced with is dealing with a stock that's losing instead of winning. What do you do? You want to get out with the least loss. If you are with a full service broker as in the example given, you would be concerned about the $600 transaction cost. You might wait a little longer for the stock to rise to make up that cost.

You wait and watch the stock **drift** a little lower, while the other stock you wanted to buy with the proceeds **rises** a little higher. If you only were concerned about a $50 round trip(Buy/Sell) cost, you probably would have sold the loser and bought the winner much quicker. You would have had little or no concern about transaction cost. Most importantly, you would have been dramatically more flexible. In fact, your transaction cost should never, ever enter your decision process when it comes time to buy or sell stocks. A low transaction cost makes this possible. A high transaction cost makes this difficult.

BANK BROKERS

I'll be specific right up front. **Don't** use banks for your brokerage needs. Especially your own bank.

The dictionary defines the word **bank** as follows:

Receptacle, Safekeeper, Keeper

This means the **absence of risk**. A place to put your money and things for safekeeping. A place where your things are kept **away** from **risk**.

The bank protects your money and valuables. The bank places your valuables in a safebox within massive vaults inside concrete bunkers with solid steel doors opened by electronic controls. When the bank gets robbed, the police and FBI swarm all over the place and mount a massive hunt for the bank robbers. Even if the authorities don't catch the thieves or catch them after they hide the money, you lose nothing because the bank's insurance will replenish the loss to the bank and you.

What if the bank goes bankrupt? You still would have no problem so long as you use a bank in the U.S. The FDIC, (Federal Deposit Insurance Corporation) guarantees against losses up to $100,000 in each separate account.

Moreover, the FDIC supervises the banks to make sure the problem is handled before the bank fails by either forcing the bank to improve its condition, taking over the bank directly or arranging a merger with a strong bank.

When you go to your bank to buy and sell stocks, mutual funds, bonds or any type of security, you are placing your money at risk in a place where risk is almost against the law. Bankers are trained to **avoid risk**, not to take it. When you use your bank for your security investments, you are mixing up two things which should be **totally separated.**

When you use your bank as your stock broker, you could be placing your bank accounts at risk. The broker at the bank has access to your bank account records. He knows what you have. Since he is on commission, he will try hard to steer you into security transactions.

His pay depends on commissions and transactions. This especially includes mutual funds. You don't ever want to make any investments in a bank other than simple CD's which really aren't investments. CD's are time deposits where the principal is like money in the bank and the interest is guaranteed for a specified time period and not subject to market conditions and manipulations.

There is another very important reason for keeping your stock brokerage business totally away from your bank. If you have a brokerage account with the bank broker and you have the misfortune of receiving a **margin call,** the broker could take **money out of your account, without your approval**. A more serious situation could occur if you should fall upon financial hard times, for whatever reason and have a judgment levied against you. Having your stocks at your bank makes it that much easier for your adversaries to find and seize your assets.

This would especially be bad for you if you also had your home mortgage at the same bank. Let's suppose that you were laid off or someone in the family has a serious illness. You just got laid off from your job but make side money from stock trading which somehow you have learned to do well.

You have fallen behind in your mortgage payments and credit card payments because you have conserved your cash to eat and fund your stock trading. And the stock trading is your only present source of income. Guess what? Your bank could seize or freeze your brokerage account real easy. It's inhouse and the bank knows what you have. Your plan to buy time until you got another job or make it big in trading just vanished in a flash.

Now, you have no income and you get behind in the payments again because this time, you have no income from trading. The bank had seized or froze the assets in your stock account. Guess what could happen? You go hungry, the bank forecloses your house and you join the homeless crowd and eat at the center for the poor. By this time, your wife probably has also left you.

Keep your investments away from your bank.

FINANCIAL PLANNERS

Financial planners are insurance agents who also act as stock brokers and mutual fund salesmen. They typically work in a small office or out of their homes. They may be called Financial Planners, Account Executives, Registered Representatives and who are probably affiliated with a local branch office of a national broker dealer.

Financial Planners often offer a valuable service as they can provide a comprehensive financial plan combining insurance, securities and other financial products. Their service should be very personal which may be good in some circumstances.

However, most financial planners work on commission, just like the brokers and must make a living. This living is made on transactions and therefore, all comments made in this book on brokers also apply to financial planners. Historically, financial planners like limited partnerships and mutual funds, annuity contracts and insurance plans. These are high commission items and the investor should be very concerned about these and especially limited partnerships which should be totally avoided.

Financial planners should generally be avoided by investors who frequently trade stocks and need to be close to the market. Here are a few reasons:

ONE: Commissions tend to be high
TWO: Services are limited due to small office
THREE: The broker is not always available and there may not be a backup person. This could present serious problems during market emergencies or immediate personal needs.

If you do prefer to work with a financial planner, use the following guidelines:

ONE: Be certain both of you have discussed and agree on your overall financial goals.

TWO: You feel very good about his broker dealer and the clearinghouse that firm uses.

THREE: Get a toll free 800 number to call the trader directly at the broker/dealer as a backup when you have a need and your financial planner is unavailable.

FOUR: Come to a clear understanding on commissions and fees to avoid misunderstandings and disputes later.

FIVE: Pick a financial planner in your local area. Never, ever use one from out of town. That would eliminate the primary reason for working with a financial planner who is supposed to provide a personal service.

SIX: Don't use a financial planner unless he also becomes your insurance agent, because that should be the primary focus in this type of relationship.

WHAT IS A CLEARINGHOUSE?

Have you heard about clearinghouses? I bet you haven't. You should be very familiar with **clearinghouses** because that's where your stocks and money are located. When you send your money to the broker, it goes directly to the clearinghouse, **not** to the broker. When you buy stocks and any other investments, your clearinghouse holds them. Think of clearinghouses as the **bank** where you have placed your investment assets. Are you now interested?

When you use a large full service broker like Merrill Lynch or Smith Barney, you don't have to worry about this. Large brokerage firms have their own clearing departments. They carry your account inhouse.

But when you use a **small** full service firm or most discount brokers, you should **worry a lot** and make sure that you feel good about the clearing firm they use. It's like picking a bank. Wouldn't you take great care about which bank you use? Your bank keeps your money and processes your checks.

The clearing firm for your broker serves no less a role. It holds your securities, processes your buy & sell orders, sends your checks to you, makes wire transfers on your instructions and more. Your broker is really no more than an **introducer** who takes your orders and relays them to the clearing house.

Are you **interested now?** The following are questions you should ask your prospective new broker before signing on with him:

1. What is the name of your Clearinghouse?
2. What are the margin rules?
3. Does your Clearinghouse provide a check writing service?
4. Is your clearinghouse insured?

Chances are that the Clearinghouse is one of the large houses such as Pershing, U.S. Trust, Fidelity, Broadcort or one of the major brokerage companies who also clear for smaller brokerage firms and discounters.

If it is unfamiliar to you, ask the broker to send you a brochure on his clearinghouse. You should also call the NASD at 202-728-8039 to request a report on the Clearinghouse company relative to any complaints and securities compliance problems. This is free and you have the right to this information. You might be surprised that there are clearinghouses with serious violations and borderline financial strength.

If you have an account with a brokerage firm and the clearinghouse goes under, **bankrupt**, shut down because of insufficient capital or any other reason, the Securities Investor Protection Corporation insures your account for cash up to $100,000 and securities up to $500,000. The problem is though, that your account becomes **frozen** sometimes up to a year. During this time, you can't buy, sell or often even take money out. You could stand by helplessly watching your stocks go way down and can't sell and lose big or you could see your stock soar but can't sell to take your profit. I have gone through one of these clearinghouse failures in real life and don't ever want to be involved with this again. The best way to prevent this potential financial disaster in your life is to be very interested in your broker's **clearinghouse** and never, ever open an account with a broker unless you feel real good about his **clearinghouse**.

HOW TO INVEST IN MUTUAL FUNDS

Trillions of Dollars are invested in nearly 5,000 mutual funds. The financial papers are full of advertisements promoting specific funds. Brokers recommend their mutual funds and this is one of the favorite sales pitches by the army of financial planners throughout the United States. How can you make money and how can you select which fund is right for you?

First, you should realize that mutual funds are securities like individual stocks. The price fluctuates as the market rises and falls and this means **risk.** A mutual fund represents a cross section of stocks a particular fund has bought consistent with a funds's specific investment policy.

Some funds are very broad and invest in hundreds of stocks in all kinds of industries. Some funds invest primarily in medical stocks. Others buy shares of small companies. Some focus on companies that are considered kind to the environment while others will buy only companies that are considered ethically proper by a specific standard. You can even invest in funds that focus on racial and religious differences.

This book does not focus on investment merits in any specific industry, company or mutual fund. There are many books and services that give this type of information. Rather, we will focus on the **how to do it** and how to avoid potential abuses. The following are specific guidelines for mutual fund investing:

ONE: Treat a mutual fund like stock. It can drop just like a stock causing you to lose hard earned money.

TWO: Get very interested and familiar with market trends and the factors that cause the market to move up and down. Mutual funds reflect market moves. In a bear market, they go down just like they go up in a rising bull market.

THREE: Buy mutual funds with the idea to sell high and buy back low. Flush down your toilet the idea that mutual funds should be bought and put in your hope chest or mattress to be forgotten.

FOUR: If you are into a dollar cost averaging program, that is you are buying a fixed Dollar amount of mutual funds in over a specific time period, such as $100 per month, place an upper Dollar limit. Consider selling when reaching this limit and the market tops out.

FIVE: Avoid mutual funds offered and managed by the large brokerage houses and banks with brokerage departments. These are typically higher commission products you are steered to and not necessarily the best for you. The bank also makes money on these funds in the role as manager and operator. There simply is too much financial incentive for the bank in selling these funds which represents a serious potential conflict of interest between seller and client.

SIX: Use only no-load or funds that allow you to switch from one kind of fund to another and between funds and cash with no commission or at a nominal transfer fee. In this instance, you hold your cash in a money-market fund or are able to electronically transfer funds to and from your bank account. This allows you to switch when market conditions indicate you should. If you are charged high commissions, you are severely discouraged to make the best of your investment Dollar.

HOW TO GET AND EVALUATE
INVESTMENT INFORMATION

Where do you get information on the companies you are interested in? When you get it, what does it mean? How can you rely on the accuracy of this information? Does it matter where you get it? What do you do with it?

These are very important questions and they will be answered herein. You may want to refer back to the chapter on **News Release Process** as it describes this process and some legal aspects of disseminating corporate information.

The following news sources are available to you:

* Direct from the company
* Brokerage firms
* Investment newsletters
* Independent research consultants
* TV and radio commentators
* Friends and fellow employees
* Electronic bulletin boards

There are three basic things you need to know about these sources for news. They are:

A. **How** to get the news
B. **What** the news really means
C. **What** do you do with the news

One of the most important tasks in evaluating investments is to get accurate information on a timely basis. Accurate means that you get **all** the information you need for decision making. Accurate also means that you receive the information from an **unbiased source** that has not altered the data in any material way. The information also has to be **accurate as of the time you received it.**

For example, would you buy a house based on the value set by the seller? No, you would ask for an independent appraisal to be sure you are getting fair value. The bank would never let you buy the house without first getting an appraisal.

Would you buy a business without **first** having an independent auditor examine the financial statements and validate that the assets are what the seller claims they are? If you had a lawyer assisting you, he would never let you buy the business unless you had first obtained the accountant's report validating the financial statement given to you by the seller.

If you applied to the bank for a loan, chances are that you would have to provide financial statements and copies of your tax returns which validate your income. Additionally, the bank probably would call your employer to confirm that you work there and you have the type of job you claim you have.

If you buy a stock, bond, mutual fund, limited partnership or any type of investment, can you think of any reason why you don't need to know a lot about these investments? Is buying an investment really that much different than buying a business or a house? Would you **buy a house on the telephone** without first looking at the house and getting an appraisal? Would you buy a company from someone calling you on the phone and one you have never heard of before? Of course you wouldn't. That would be crazy.

A broker calls and tells you to buy 1000 shares of XYZ at $10 before **you** have had a chance to see anything on the company to validate the information he gave you. He offers to send you some information on the company. How do you know that the broker has the **right** and **current** information?

Did he get it from the company directly? Did he hear it on the TV? Did he learn about it in a research report? If so, **when** was that report written and by **whom**? Do any of these people have a potential financial gain by your buying this stock?

Of course! The commission, their daily bread. Would you send out your hard earned $10,000 based on just a phone call and without doing any checking?

You would be surprised how many people do just this. The investment sounds so good. How could you possibly not **rush** in your $10,000 right away when you have the chance to **double it or even triple** it in no time at all? There is always a sense of urgency as the stock is likely to go up the very next day and you want to get aboard before that happens.

How many people lose their shirts by not checking out the facts by getting them from reliable and unbiased sources? After reading this book and this section, is there any chance you'll be one of them? Now, let's get to the specifics. **Where** and how to get reliable information.

DIRECT FROM THE COMPANY

The most reliable information usually comes directly from the company. It is written by management, reviewed often by the company attorney, in many cases subject to government regulations and in the case of financial data, usually audited by independent external auditors. While this does not guarantee complete honesty and accuracy, it's about the best you can do.

Receiving information directly from the company avoids the interpretation, analyses and potentially **biased opinion of intermediaries whose interests may be adverse to yours.** It is preferred that you, the investor **who pays and are at risk,** form your conclusion and base your decisions on the best facts available. These facts are usually from the company. That does not preclude your receiving and using analysts reports, getting opinions from brokers and advisors or anyone, for that matter. While these can offer valuable leads, they should be validated with facts based on information you consider most reliable.

The following are the basic reports you can receive from the company:

THE ANNUAL REPORT summarizes the prior year business, gives the financial details, tells you what the company makes and often something about its future plans.

THE PROXY STATEMENT is sent out as part of the annual meeting notice. This lists the directors and officers along with their backgrounds and compensation, how many shares they own and proposals to be voted on at the annual meeting.

REGULATORY REPORTS are sent by the Company to the SEC. These are the 10-K for the prior fiscal year and the 10-Q for each quarter. The 10K must be made available prior to the 90th day after the close of the company's fiscal year. The 10-Q must be issued within 45 days after the close of the prior quarter. These reports are required and mandatory to comply with securities laws and regulations.

PRESS RELEASES are issued by the company when it announces the financial results and news of major events such as new business contracts, executive appointments, mergers and other major events like bankruptcies, stock splits etc.

The procedure for receiving these and keeping up to date is simple and you don't need anyone else doing this for you. It's much better if you do this yourself because then, you are the person who gets it directly.

Just pick up the phone or write to the company's Director of Investor Relations or Chief Financial Officer requesting the *investor's package*. This typically contains the Annual Report, the 10-Q and 10-K and possibly a company profile along with the last few releases. **Request** that you be placed on the **FAX list** for press releases. This gives you the news immediately, the same time as the brokers, editors and investment professionals. If you don't have a fax machine, invest $200 and get one. If you are into investments, this should be a basic requirement because it assures you receiving information on a timely basis and avoids your losing this advantage to others. If you don't want to get a fax, ask to be placed on a mailing list for everything.

RESEARCH REPORTS FROM BROKERS

Brokerage companies write research reports to assist the brokers in marketing the stocks recommended by their firms. These are sales tools and should be viewed as such. These reports usually have lots of information including financial data and can be useful as background material.

But never, ever forget that these are written by analysts paid by the brokerage firms that make money by selling stocks through their brokers who get paid commission every time there is a transaction. The very purpose of these reports is to get you to buy the stocks recommended in them to generate commissions. Look at them like sales brochures and advertising materials.

You can get good and valuable information from these research reports. But you should always remember that they are written for purposes **often adverse to your interest.**

For example, if the brokerage house were the investment banker for a company and in that process received restricted shares or other securities as part of the fee, these securities must be sold at some future time. What happens if that time has arrived and the brokerage firm needs to sell them out of its inventory? What happens if the brokerage firm is a current investment banker for a company and needs to get the stock price up? What would happen if the brokerage firm advises a mutual fund or a big pension fund? There now is a need to sell a large block of a particular stock and the fund is worried that the stock will fall if it is placed on the market?

Here comes the research report with glowing forecasts for the company and paints a bright future. The research department issues this report with a **Strong Buy** recommendation. It's Monday morning and time for the weekly Research Director's conference call to all 1000 offices throughout the United States. He says "**buy** stock XYC".

Call your clients and tell them about this outstanding investment opportunity. All clients should **own** this stock. Send your Clients the research report so they can see how great this thing really is.

Right away, the army of 10,000 brokers get on their phones and call their clients. Everybody gets fired up. The research director issues a press release announcing that his firm has placed Company XYC on its **Focus List** which shows up in the financial press. The clients see this and guess what? They buy the stock when their broker calls. Maybe it was a good investment based on its own merits, at that price. Maybe not. But the main reason for the research report was to move stock out for the benefit of the brokerage firm. If it also benefited the investors, the folk like us, that was secondary in importance.

Should you use research reports prepared by brokerage firms? Of course. If you have an interest in a particular stock or industry, these can provide valuable information. Just be sure you use it as **background information only.** You should be careful that you don't buy the recommended stock at its very high to see it drop right after you buy it. Sure, it probably could go to even higher prices later but later could be months away. Why not wait on the sidelines and evaluate the situation?

This gives you the chance to learn much more about the company while the money remains in **your** hands, earning interest. You can easily check the stock's price pattern by looking at a simple stock chart which often is included in the research report. If it isn't, ask your broker for one. If the broker doesn't have one, you can get it in your local library. Or, for less than $50 per month and if you have a computer, you can get a stock chart from any number of technical charting services.

If you invest in stocks, you should allocate a budget for your independent research so that you can intelligently evaluate opportunities. The **savings** by using a discount broker instead of a full service broker will **more than pay for this research.** Remember, if you buy a business, you know you must do a fair amount of due diligence.

Buying stocks is no different. The research report from a brokerage company should be only one input to your decision. Be sure it is **not** the only information source.

You should always remember that if you missed this opportunity, there will be a next one. There is no substitute for reliable and verifiable information. However, you don't want to become an analyst and spend your entire life researching and not investing. Then, you become a student instead of an investor. It's important to find a reasonable balance between shooting from the hip and quickly jumping into unknown situations to being a student who never acts on any information.

INVESTMENT LETTERS

Investment Letters are reports usually written by persons outside the brokerage industry. There are hundreds of "Letters" written by people and companies. All kinds of situations are covered. One *letter* makes stock recommendations based on astrology which reflects the positions of the planets relative to the Earth and the stars. Others emphasize how much corporate insiders buy and sell. Some focus on small companies, one letter reviews medical stocks and the list goes on. A few investment letters review other investment letters and give summaries and excerpts from them.

There are publication firms that produce as many as 30 different investment letters in Occasionally, a really interesting one shows up. If you received an airmail letter postmarked in Lichtenstein, Europe inviting you to join a select and mysterious group connected with the inside track in Switzerland and high international finance, watch out. This letter was published by a company in Florida as part of a papermill producing about 30 monthly investment letters.

You can get very good ideas from investment letters. Just be sure you check it all out for yourself and realize that the newsletter writer could benefit if you buy the stock recommended. Check the disclosures and the fine print at the bottom of the page. A few report writers get paid by the company recommended to *recommend* that stock. The value of this recommendation is far less than the recommendation made by a totally independent analyst.

You can get **trial** subscriptions for short time periods which give you the opportunity to evaluate the track record before subscribing for a whole year. It's always a good idea to **try a letter** out before shelling out anywhere from $50 to $500 for a one year subscription. It is especially a good idea to track a particular letter's performance record before buying stocks recommended therein.

TV, RADIO
AND
FINANCIAL PRESS

"Honey, I heard about this great company on the radio driving from work today. Should we buy some stock tomorrow morning?"

No. Absolutely not. Buying a stock or any investment right away based on what you hear on the radio, TV or read in the financial press immediately could be a bad mistake. You should make it a cardinal rule never to buy any investment recommended especially on the radio or TV without a very thorough **and independent evaluation**.

The safest approach would be to simply never listen to these types of programs, especially the talk host shows featuring a commentator who focuses on low priced stocks. Programs like Wall Street Week and the Nightly Business Report are OK because they focus on general financial news, and commentary on economic events. But even here, when you hear specific stocks recommended even by the most respected guests, you should take great care.

The reasons are simple:

* The commentator may be paid to promote the stock by the company.
* The commentator may represent a brokerage firm with inventory to sell.
* The commentator may be one link in a **bear raid** or **short** network.

Study has shown that stocks recommended on prime time national financial host shows often rise during the **prior** week and drop right after the program. This also applies to major articles in the written press. Why is this?

First, the commentator knows which stocks he'll recommend. If he is a broker or is affiliated with a brokerage firm, he and his clients will buy these stocks **prior** to his appearance. If the guest is a newsletter editor, his subscribers and his inner circle clients, will know, in advance, what his top stock picks are for that month and which he is likely to recommend. They will buy extra shares. These purchases are generally for a quick trade rather than for investments.

When a financial magazine does a major story on a company management, interviews and photo sessions usually precede the publication date. Persons in the **inner circle know this** and invariable, some brokers learn this too.

They will call their clients telling them that there is a rumor of a major article coming out imminently and it's time to buy more shares for a quick extra profit.

By the time the guest commentator mentions his stock and the magazine gets to the news stand, an **above average** number of shares will have been bought, as evidenced by rising volume and price during the prior week or two. Then, the price and volume rises even more right after the event because you and others like you rush out to buy the stock.

But, the stock you bought will be the very same stock bought by the people who bought it prior to the show. They **now are selling to you.** In fact, they may even be shorting the stock, that is selling shares they don't even own because they know that the stock will likely drop in a week or two. That's the expectation, based on history.

Have you ever heard the expression **"buy on the rumor and sell on the news?"** That's one of the tools in the traders toolbox of tricks. You, the investor are the mark in this game. The traders, brokers and the commentators often take advantage of this Wall Street game.

In these situations, they have a significant advantage over you because of their high level access to the information flow. The commentators and their network have an extraordinary good access to investment information.

How does the commentator get paid? Read on. You are about to learn something few people know. That's the purpose of this book. To tell you what goes on **inside Wall Street** and to give you a decent chance to make money.

Let's take the example of a well known guest on a prime time financial panel show. The host asks him what stocks he likes now and he mentions just two or three with his reasons. Why did he pick just these few?

The guest is **Director of Research** for a brokerage firm. The firm is named but often, the introducer does not mention what kind of company it is. In this case it is a small brokerage firm. Rarely, if ever mentioned is the fact that this firm may be on a retainer as **investment banker** for the company being recommended.

Now, let's recall from a previous chapter the role of the investment banker. His job is to enhance the value of his client's stock and assist in mergers and acquisitions. In this particular instance, the commentator was referred to the client company by an investor relations firm also on retainer from the client company. Moreover, there is a referral fee structure in place between the investor relations consultant and the investment banker.

Why did the company retain these people? Because the company was unable, through natural means to get the stock price up.

The investor relations consultant made it clear, right up front, that if he were hired, he would bring in an investment banker for a nominal fee . What would be the role of this investment banker? Since he frequently appears on national investment talk shows, chances are good that he would **recommend** the client company as an excellent investment opportunity.

So far, the investor relations consultant and the investment banker have made money. Money paid by the client company in fees. Money made by the investment banker acting in his brokerage capacity selling more shares and collecting commissions.

Now, we come to the event. The program. You and millions hear about this great little company with a wonderful new product and how good an investment it is. Some of you rush out to buy the stock and the price rises. Guess what? The investment banker is also a **market maker** in this stock. He accumulated shares in this company **prior** to the show. Now, he'll start selling to you at the **ask** price after raising the **ask** price a little. The investment banker, now acting in his role as a broker/dealer making a market in the stock, is making a killing in spreads, markups and commissions through his retail brokerage department. Guess what? The investor relations consultant just happens to be a favored client of the investment banker, This gives him an outstanding opportunity for quick profits by participating in this situation. He bought **before** the TV show and sold right afterwards, when the stock spurted up for a day or two.

Could the company he recommended be a good investment? Possibly. But rarely at the time you hear it mentioned on a major program. The price at that time usually is too high for the reasons just given. What do you do with the information you hear on the program? The same as you would do with any input you receive from anyone when it comes to business.

You check it out and get the facts from sources **you know** are **reliable** and **accurate**. You look at the chart to evaluate the trading pattern and trend. If you still think it's a great investment, then by all means buy it.

But don't buy it until you looked at the chart. If you buy the stock when you first hear about it, especially on a prime time TV program, the chances are at least 90% that you would buy that stock at a high level and that it will drop during the next several weeks. Why not wait for that drop?

If you are so motivated that you feel you have to buy that stock right away, buy no more than half of what you planned to buy. If it goes up after you buy it, you make money. If it drops, wait until the drop ends and it starts to rise a little again. Then buy the rest. You win here too because you limited the loss if it dropped and you decided it was a mistake. If you confirmed through your independent evaluation that the stock was indeed a good investment and the stock still dropped after the program, then you reduced your average cost by waiting to buy the other half.

This is called **hedging your bet** and not being greedy. You should always remember that a hedge protects you against the wolves while not being too greedy can keep you away from the slaughterhouse.

When you hear someone promoting a stock on TV, radio or in a publication, always, without fail, assume that someone wants to sell something to you he already has. In this case, it's a stock he already owns and wants to sell to you at a price higher than he paid.

FRIENDS AND RELATIVES

"Honey, cousin Harry called yesterday telling us to buy stock XYZ. He said that he has **inside** information and that it'll **fly** real soon. He also told me to tell you that you can't tell this to anyone."

"Sweetie, our Son just called to tell me his friend told him that the company he is working for is doing real good. He works in the shipping department and he noticed that last month there was a dramatic increase in shipments and that this means business is up. Should we buy some of the stock?"

"Darling, my boss at work told me about this stock that's about to fly. You think we should buy some?"

Be very careful here. You are entering poisoned waters where there is little chance of winning. If you buy and lose, you'll blame your friend, your relative or your wife's boss which could lead to strained relations. If you win, you have placed yourself into a position of debt to those people. The time will surely come when they'll call in their marker. Probably at the worst possible time. Meanwhile, it would have opened the need for frequent conversations between you and them on financial matters which usually is a very bad idea between friends, relatives and especially bosses and fellow workers.

Is there anything wrong with checking out these leads? Absolutely not! By all means look into these leads. Just remember, the information you got could be bad news as easy as good news. Let's look at your son's friend who noticed a dramatic increase in shipment from his company's shipping department. Did this mean that the company's business is up or that the company sold left over inventory at a price below its cost?

If the latter, that would be very bad for the stock as it could lead to a loss for the quarter due to inventory write-downs. A shipping clerk usually wouldn't know about this. All he knows is that more boxes are going out the back door.

What should you do about these leads? Check them out if you have the time and resources. They actually could lead to something worthwhile. But keep the results to yourself. If the result is bad news and you tell your friend or your boss, they probably won't believe it and hold it against you. If the news is good, then they will start to rely on **you** for information about **their** investments and companies. Every time they hear something, they'll ask you to check it out. This costs you time, money and worse yet, aggravation that will surely come. The answer is to **stay away** from these situations. Period!

ELECTRONIC BULLETIN BOARDS

Millions of people use the information superhighway by accessing services like PRODIGY, America Online, CompuServe, Internet and others. These services offer bulletin boards on all imaginable subjects. Social issues, personal ads, religion, health and yes, money and stocks. Anyone subscribing to these services can post notices and respond to others on the bulletin boards, within the framework of the rules. These rules are very loose. A female can seek a new lesbian companionship sorted by ZIP codes and someone can tell millions of people about a great stock. This can be lots of fun and everyone is encouraged to use these services if you have a computer. Today, millions own computers all over the world and these are connected to each other through your telephone.

Let's log on this information superhighway and go to the **stocks** bulletin board. You browse and find all kinds of interesting information. Like someone telling the world about a wonderful company that's deeply undervalued and that will triple this year for sure.

The bulletin notice tells you about new contracts and profits just ahead. Watch out! This person could be an investor who is stuck with thousands of shares and wants to get the price up so he can sell.

He could be a broker looking for business or a person just like yourself who has found a stock he really likes and want to share with the world. All these people have two things in common:

1. They all want to get the stock up.
2. You don't know who or what they are.

What should you do? The rule here is the same as for leads you hear on TV, see in the paper or hear from your friends. **Check it out thoroughly before you leap into cyberspace stocks.**

TEN RULES
FOR
INVESTMENT SUCCESS

We have in this book examined the inner and far reaches of the world of investments and securities. We have seen how it works in a system based mainly on the transaction system where the professional's income is based on the number of transactions. We have learned that there is an inherent and basic conflict of interest built into the system that places you, the investor at an unfair disadvantage. Clearly, the odds are against the average investor in the system as it stands today.

This chapter will consider all that has been covered in this book and present ten basic rules for investor survival **and** success. These rules are simple, fundamental and very easy to follow. Adherence to these rules is critical. If you follow these guidelines, you will not only avoid potential serious financial loss, but you will dramatically increase your odds for making serious money.

ONE: Research adequately any information on investments recommended to you. Make sure you verify the information directly from the company. Don't ever act on any recommendation received from any broker paid by transaction commission alone. In each instance, check his information for accuracy, timeliness and source.

TWO: Separate the transactions from the source of investment information. This virtually eliminates a potential conflict of interest while dramatically reducing your transaction costs. It also takes transaction out as a consideration in the investment decision.

THREE: Use a deep discount broker when possible. This will save you money, time and grief. It certainly could make your investment decisions much easier. The use of a discount broker puts you, the investor, in the drivers seat and places you in full charge of your investments. You will be more informed, be more careful and spend more time monitoring your investments. This is your money and your money deserves your quality attention. The use of a low cost deep discount broker takes transaction cost out of the buy/sell decision.

FOUR: Never use any bank as your broker. Your safe and guaranteed money should always be kept apart from your risk money.

FIVE: Never use a discretionary account with any broker. This is an account where you give the broker written authorization to trade your account without your approval in advance for each transaction. Discretionary accounts give the broker the opportunity to trade excessively to generate more commissions. This is called churning and is against the rules. However, when this happens and it is identified, you, the investor have already lost your money.

SIX: Never buy any investment product from a cold caller on the telephone. You don't know that person, he may be calling from a city 3000 miles away in a large fancy office or just across the town in a one room loft boiler room.

SEVEN: Use a margin account only after you fully understand how it works and its additional risks and potential rewards. When you do use one and there are times you should, use it for near term trading. Never for longer term investing.

EIGHT: File a complaint and compensation request promptly with your broker after realizing you have not been dealt with fairly. Specific procedures are given in the chapter *What to do When You Get Into Trouble*. Don't be timid. **Go for it.**

NINE: Don't get involved with your relatives and close friends in recommending or researching investments. If you must, set up clear ground rules before getting involved.

TEN: If after reading this book you think that stocks aren't for you, the book was well worth it. It could have saved you from making costly mistakes. While you won't get rich on 5% passbook interest, you also won't go broke losing your money. Don't feel bad. Many people should not be in stocks or any investment for many reasons. One important reason for staying out of the stock market is that you don't want to allocate the right priority to manage your investments. This is a personal and an OK choice. If you don't want to spend serious time managing your investments, the best program is to have no investment program at all. Putting this in a different way. Don't get into anything you can't or don't want to manage. To say this in another way, if you can't do it right, don't do it at all. A half hearted effort with your own investments can be one of the worst and costliest mistakes of your life.

There is nothing more frightful than ignorance in action
Johann Wolfgang von Goethe

WHAT TO DO
WHEN
YOU GET IN TROUBLE

You lost a significant amount of money taking your brokers advise. You have a dispute with your broker on a trade. You received faulty information from the company and you acted upon it. You made the mistake of buying a stock from a penny stock broker that pestered you on the phone. You bought an investment from your bank thinking it was guaranteed. You don't like your present broker and just want to move the account to another brokerage firm. These are situations faced by many investors.

Should you grin and bear it and let it go? If you sincerely believe that you have been wronged and have good justification for a real complaint, you should **not let it go**. You should fight back and make a strong effort to recover some of what you lost or resolve the problem, whatever it might be.

Let's go to the broker first. You **listened to him and lost money**. You feel that he recommended too many inappropriate trades and it seems that you made less money than he made on commissions. Alternately, you lost a lot while he made out real well on the commissions from your trades. What are your rights?

FIRST: Your broker has an obligation under NASD suitability rules to recommend securities suitable to your financial situation. Failure to adhere to this rule subjects him and his firm to financial responsibility for your loss and you may have recourse for recovery.

SECOND: Excessive trading may be considered **Churning** which is against NASD rules and subject to disciplinary action and compensation to client.

Do you need a lawyer to deal with this? No. In fact you may be better off if you try to resolve this on your own without an attorney. If you want the advice of a lawyer to guide you, that's fine. Just make sure you consult with an attorney specializing in securities law and is familiar with arbitration procedures within the brokerage industry. The following are steps you can take on your own.

ONE: Find out who is the president of the brokerage company. You may have to make several long distance calls to get this information or even go to the library and look it up in the business section. Also get his FAX number because you will need it later. Under no circumstance should you settle for anyone except the President, Executive Vice President or the Managing Director and you must have a name for these titles. Going to the top is part of the process and critical to succeed in your effort.

SECOND: Write a letter, addressed to this person and send it by Certified Mail with return receipt requested. In this letter give an accurate account of what you believe has happened, state how much money you lost and request to be compensated. Add 50% to the amount you think you lost because in reality, your loss is much bigger than you think. Loss of interest you would have received if you had the money in a bank and loss of opportunity by not being placed in more appropriate investments are just two reasons. Give him a date of 15 days after your sending it. At the bottom of the letter, add the words: CC: NASD Compliance Division. Then, send the copy to:
NASD COMPLIANCE DIVISION
NASD, 1735 K Street, NW Washington DC 20006.

When the 15 days have passed and you haven't heard anything, which is likely, send a FAX to that very same person advising him that he has 72 hours to respond or you will file a formal complaint with the NASD and the SEC.

Make sure that you place CC: NASD and SEC Compliance Director at the bottom of this fax and indeed fax or mail it Certified to those officers.

Chances are good that you now will hear something from someone. Don't expect too much because the brokerage firm will try to make you feel good and delay anything further you might do. They want to buy time and gather information about your account. They will do everything possible to give you a runaround, hoping you will go away. This is the **wearing out process.**

When the 72 hours pass and you still haven't heard anything or anything meaningful, write a Certified Letter with return receipt requested to the NASD Compliance Director. In the first paragraph, summarize clearly your complaint, that you sincerely tried to resolve the matter but that you have not had any meaningful response.

In the second paragraph, request that the NASD immediately initiate an investigation in this matter. At the bottom of this letter, write CC: SEC, Compliance Director, Washington, DC and actually mail him a copy. Be sure you attach to this letter copies of all correspondence and faxes you have sent to the brokerage company.

Next, you should send another FAX to the brokerage firm president. You should clearly state that if there is not a reasonable response within 72 hours, you will forward the entire file to the Editor of the Business Section of your largest local newspaper with a copy to the Editor of the Wall Street Journal. Be sure to attach the letter you sent to the SEC and NASD. This is very important.

While you have been doing these things, a file has gradually been created at the brokerage firm, the NASD and now, at the SEC. The brokerage firm is starting to incur some cost and beginning to feel that this case may cause problems and might not go away by ignoring it.

This is very good. **Good for you.** You want to keep up the pressure, cause them to incur more expenses and above all, believe that you really mean business. You want the brokerage firm to know that the file is also building at the NASD and SEC.

The brokerage firm's compliance department might have by now received a letter of inquiry from the NASD and the SEC. That would be great for you.

Chances are good that you will be offered a settlement just to keep from getting bad publicity for the brokerage firm and save potential legal expenses.

If the settlement is ridiculously low or represents only a token payment to get rid of you, reject it immediately. Send a letter to the brokerage firm advising it of your rejection and clearly state that you will proceed with the processing of your complaint with the authorities within 5 days if a reasonable settlement offer has not been received by that date.

If you get an offer near what you want, respond **in writing** with an offer somewhat higher. Clearly state that your offer is good for only 10 days after which it expires and that you will continue the full process available under the law. They'll probably accept, because by that time, the brokerage firm has spent serious time and money and wants to put it to a stop.

You also have become a problem in the executive office and you slowly have worn them down. But, they will only give in if you persist. You must take steps to make sure **they know** you won't go away. Don't be timid about this. Be aggressive. The worse they think of you, the better chance you have of winning. In this rare instance, becoming a big nuisance can be a very good thing.

Now, lets assume you haven't succeeded. This is the time to send one last letter to the Brokerage firm's president. Remember, always send correspondence to the same person. You want to make sure you have become a nuisance. This last letter simply tells him that you will refer the entire matter to your securities attorney and it will be out of your hands unless there is a serious attempt to settle the matter. Don't mail it. Always FAX it. If you don't have a FAX machine, go to the nearest store that has one.

Guess what you accomplished all by yourself at very little cost and in a short time? You either recovered some or all of your lost money or established a solid case full with paperwork for your lawyer. That gives him a headstart and saves you money. Your only cost thus far is a little time and telephone calls sending the faxes.

Up to this point, you did it all by yourself without a lawyer. However, if you didn't succeed, seek the advice of a lawyer experienced in securities law.

Now, let's go to less serious problems, like delays in getting your account transferred, questionable trades and other situations about your account.

If you have **questions about the price you got** on your trade, call your broker and request a **trade and time** report during the day your trade took place. This report gives price and volume for each transaction of your stock that day and is supposed to tell you if you received the right price for your own trade. This means work for the broker and you may have to insist that he gets it for you. Be sure to request this report in writing. Otherwise, you won't know if he is just giving you information you want to hear to get him off the hook.

If you have any hassles with this, say goodbye and hang up. Then call back and ask to speak with the manager. If you don't get satisfactory answers, go back to the procedure we went through and start with the President.

Transferring an account should be a very easy process. All you have to do is to fill out the transfer request given to you by the new broker, attach a copy of your most recent statement and give it back to your new broker. This is a computer to computer transfer process designed to take no more than two weeks unless there are problems with the account. If there is delay beyond two weeks, call the manager of your **former** brokerage office and ask him to give you the status of the transfer.

Follow up on this with him and the new broker. **Be relentless. Become a nuisance** if necessary. Your old broker doesn't want to lose your business and he may think that a delay might cause you to change your mind.

If you put the pressure on, like calling every day or even personally stopping by the office, the manager will personally expedite the transfer just to get rid of you. Another effective means of making a nuisance of yourself is to send daily faxes to the brokerage office.

Regulations require that each communication coming and going must be logged and filed in a special file called **Complaints**. This takes time and time is money. The branch manager also prefers to keep the **office complaint file** empty. Less important but still noteworthy is that fax paper is not free which means that your daily faxes are costing the office. Most of your life, you want to avoid becoming a nuisance. This is one of those **rare exceptions** when becoming a **nuisance** is a very good thing.

When you have a problem, take charge of your solution. It will make you feel good about yourself while accomplishing an important and very vital task. It's about *Getting back at the Thieves on Wall Street.*

I keep six honest serving men. They taught me all I knew. Their names are What, Why, When, How, Who and Where
Rudyard Kipling

They have sown the wind, and they shall reap the whirlwind
Hosea 8:7, The Holy Bible

PRESCRIPTION
TO
CHANGE THE SYSTEM

This book has focused on the present system, how the odds are heavily stacked against the individual and presented ways of improving these odds. Is there a better way? Can the present system be improved?

Yes, there is opportunity for dramatic improvement and yes, it can be done. The question is whether the titans of business and government will face up to their responsibilities to implement change. This is a difficult situation because the heads of companies who would have to initiate change would likely suffer by implementing it. Why? Because these are the people who benefit from the present system. A system which is structured to extract money from the millions of investors to fill the coffers of a few.

What about the government? Is it not the role of the government to look after the interests of the public? After all, is that not why we have regulators like the Securities and Exchange Commission(SEC). Of course. But the trend has been to decrease the role of government's interference in private business. Government agencies have been placed under strong pressure to decrease regulations and foster a free market place. Therefore, there is not much hope, for the near term anyway, to expect the government to help the individual and average investor. Frankly, we probably are better off if the government stays away as the quality of government service has deteriorated over the years and that trend is accelerating. It has also been observed over the years that more meddling by the government bureaucrats usually makes a poor situation worse.

Is there hope? Yes. This hope comes from the market-place. It comes from you and I. What we do with our investment Dollars. How we invest them, which services we use and which services we refuse to use. The actions we take can have a profound impact on the system and dictate change for the better.

If all Americans followed just the ten simple steps in the chapter *Ten Rules For Investor Success* and used the principles presented in this book, the system would be cleaned up real fast. The penny stock brokers would starve. The *tree shakers* would run out of trees to shake. The *boiler rooms* would shut down. The SEC could even reduce its budget because there would be less need to police the industry. The brokerage firms could improve quality of research and recommendations by focusing more on real corporate fundamentals rather than the stimulation of sales to move inventory shares or meet sales quotas.

I propose a few basic changes in this final chapter. After all, it is unfair to be critical without offering specific ways to solve the problems. The following are specific actions that can be taken by the securities industry which could go a long way toward improving the system.

ONE: The **Securities Industry** should adopt new guidelines for hiring brokers. There should be a greater focus on background and integrity than how much business volume the broker brings to the firm. The compensation schedule should be restructured. The broker should be paid a nominal salary sufficient for basic life and the opportunity to make a huge income based on performance for the clients and the total Dollar value in the broker's accounts. This rewards the broker for performing well for the client while also doing well for the firm. Importantly, this takes away the incentive to create all kinds of schemes to generate high income through short term speculations and churning the accounts.

TWO: The **government** should reward investors for investing in America, rather than punish investors. This can easily be accomplished by changing the tax code. Taxing investments is like punishing a person for placing his money at risk helping to stimulate America's business. The removal of this regressive tax would go a long way to encourage individuals toward greater investment which would lead to **more business** for the securities industry.

The loss of taxes from the capital gains tax is more than offset by the increased profits generated by industry which is taxed. It also is a proven fact that more capital available for industry leads to more jobs which in turn leads to more wages and hence, more personal taxes on wages. The individual benefits in two important ways from this proposed tax code revision. He keeps more of his investment gains while having the opportunity for increased job security at higher wages. During the past ten years, job security and wages have dramatically dropped for millions of Americans as a result of the restructuring we have seen during this period.

It is estimated that about 8 million Americans have been restructured out of their professions and careers prematurely during the recent few years. These people pay dramatically lower taxes or even no tax after the ax falls on their job at age 55. The annual tax revenue loss to the government from this item alone is estimated at about $50 billion per year. This loss is based on an estimated personal income loss of about $160 billion annually which has a direct negative impact on the economy. If the government would accomplish just this simple tax code revision, most of Washington could go on vacation for the rest of the year and we would be better off.

THREE: You, the individual investor and small business owner could simply follow the guidelines given in this book. The securities industry would become restructured very quickly to survive in some form. You, the investor, would force the securities industry to recognize and adjust itself to the needs of the market place.

These are **Three simple recommendations**. One for the Industry. One for the government and one for the market place which is you, the investor.

Could it happen? Very easily if the American public took seriously the principles and information presented in this book.

I did my part. I wrote the book.

The world hates change, yet it is the only thing that has brought progress.

Charles F. Kettering

Thought is the blossom; language the bud; action is the fruit behind it.

Ralph Waldo Emerson

GLOSSARY

It is important to clearly understand key words and terms used in **brokerspeak** as an added measure of defense against the *Thieves on Wall Street* The terms listed in this glossary are thoroughly explained in this book. However, it is useful to have a reference handy and even occasionally browse through this list. A blank page is intentionally added for your convenient use in writing in additional terms you might come across.

ASK: Price paid when buying stocks
BID: Price received when selling stocks
BOILER ROOM: A brokerage firm using high pressure telemarketing sales people as brokers.
COMMISSION: Money paid to broker for transactions
COMPLIANCE: Adherence to rules
DERIVATIVE: A synthetic financial product linked to a real financial number such as interest rates, index, stock price or commodity future price
DUE DILIGENCE: Effort to evaluate financial products
DJI: Dow Jones Industrial Averages represent an index of 30 specific stocks on the NYSE. The stocks are picked to represent quality and a cross section of industries.
INSIDE INFORMATION: Significant information known only to key corporate officials and not allowed to be given anyone else prior to the official release to the outside world
INSIDE TRADER: Person having knowledge of significant information about a company that has not been disclosed to the outside world. This person can be a corporate officer, consultant, editor or relative of these. This person must adhere to specific rules when buying and selling securities.

IPO: Initial Public Offering

INVESTMENT BANKING: Raising money through stock and bond offerings and assisting companies in mergers, acquisitions, restructuring and bankruptcies

MARGIN ACCOUNT: Buying securities on credit using the securities purchased as collateral

MARGIN CALL: Demand by broker for additional cash when securities bought on margin fall below specified minimums. Failure to respond with the required additional cash normally causes the broker to **sell out** sufficient stock to cover the margin call. The broker can sell out the client's entire portfolio at a huge loss.

MARKET: The general market represented by the Dow Jones Industrial Average (DJI)

MARKET MAKER: Brokerage firm buying and selling stock for its own account

MEMBER FIRM: Brokerage firm member of the NYSE and NASD

NASD: National Association of Securities Dealers

NASDAQ: National Association of Securities Dealers Automated Quotation System

NIKKEI: Tokyo Stock Exchange Stock Index

NYSE: New York Stock Exchange

OPTION: The right to buy or sell a stock on or before a future specified date at a set price. An option is a derivative product.

PENNY STOCKS: Low priced and low quality stocks typically under $1 per share

QUOTRON: Computer screen on broker's desk displaying stock prices and a host of financial information

SEC: Securities and Exchange Commission

SHORT SELLING: Sale of borrowed stock and the repurchase of same stock to return to original owner, hope fully at a lower price to profit from a declining stock

STOCK BROKER: Person licensed to buy & sell securities on behalf of investors

STOCK EXCHANGE: Place, such as the NYSE, where stocks are bought and sold in an auction environment
TRADER: Person trading stocks short term
TRANSACTION: Process of buying and selling
WALL STREET: Wherever stocks and financial instruments are traded, including the New York Stock Exchange, NASDAQ, Chicago Futures, Tokyo Exchange

HOW TO KEEP UP
WITH
THE THIEVES

The publisher and author sincerely hope that this book has made a difference, however small, in your investment thinking. That was the purpose of this book. To bring forth those things that were hidden in the corners of the investment community.

The securities industry, as are most industries, is subject to change over time. Sometimes change is for the better. Often it is for the worse. Whether change is good or bad also depends on individual circumstances. It is important therefore, to keep up with significant changes.

Equally important is to maintain awareness of the latest in scams, schemes and just interesting happenings that go on in the securities industry. New developments occur nearly every month. Recently, we heard about the 28 year old trader destroying the oldest bank in the world with his $1 billion trading loss. The Justice Department's **investigation** into the alleged NASDAQ price fixing and two brokerage firms manipulating prices by trading between themselves for extra profit with the head of one actually going to jail. Not only can this be useful to the individual investor, but it often can be amusing and entertaining.

To give the chance of keeping up with this industry, the publisher has created a monthly newsletter titled *Keeping up with the Thieves*.

If you thought this book was worthwhile, then you will want to receive this monthly newsletter. The price is a nominal $39.95 for a full year. This also includes the privilege of sending questions to the editor and receiving a written answer.

Please fill in the coupon below or a copy thereof to receive your monthly *Keeping Up With The Thieves*.

_____

_____**YES**, I want to receive *Keeping Up With The Thieves*, a monthly newsletter with the privilege to send in written questions and receive written answers.

_____**PLACE** me on your mailing list for occasional publications relating to the practices in the world of investments. This is free.

NAME: _____
ADDRESS: _____
CITY: _____
STATE: _____ **ZIP:** _____
TEL: _____ **FAX** _____

Please send this or a copy hereof and make check payable to:

Discovery Group Inc.
1280 Terminal Way, Suite 3
Reno, Nevada 89502